KT-522-887

17

A
T

WITHDRAWN FROM
THE LIBRARY

KA 0032163 X

TY OF
STER

PERFORMANCES: DYNAMICS OF A DANCE GROUP

Performances: Dynamics of a Dance Group

EDITH COPE

LEPUS BOOKS
LONDON 1976

To the Members of

Movable Workshop

October 1973–April 1974

KING ALFRED'S COLLEGE
WINCHESTER

793.3
COP   66404

Copyright © 1976 Lepus Books
(An associate company of Henry Kimpton Ltd)

All rights reserved. No part of this publication may be
reproduced, stored in a retrieval system, or transmitted
in any form or by any means, electronic, mechanical,
photocopying, recording or otherwise, without the prior
permission of the publishers.

ISBN 0 86019 029 3

Typesetting by Malvern Typesetting Services Ltd
and printed in Great Britain at
the University Printing House, Cambridge
(Euan Phillips, University Printer)

ACKNOWLEDGEMENTS

I should like to express my gratitude to Mollie Abbott, Principal of Dunfermline College, to Jean Carroll, Assistant Principal, and to the Governors of the College, for perceiving the research potential in the formation of *Movable Workshop,* for granting the funds for the enquiry, and for making available facilities for the production of questionnaires, pamphlets and the final manuscript.

I should like to express my gratitude to the Governors of the Scottish Ballet Company for their agreement to the participation of members of the *Movable Workshop* company in the research.

Above all, I am deeply grateful to Stuart Hopps, Geoffrey McNab and all members of the *Movable Workshop* Company October 1973–April 1974. Their patient collaboration, their humour and courage in exposing themselves at a professionally challenging period to the extra demands of a research enquiry, have made this study possible. As a tribute to their uncomplaining tolerance, I dedicate to them the ensuing work.

CONTENTS

1

BEGINNINGS

The Genesis of Movable Workshop
and of the Research

In front of the grey drapes a young man is sitting, one leg nonchalantly crossed. His grey suit is orthodox, impeccable. His hooded eyes, melancholy in a droll face, are scanning the *Police Gazette*. From the side, in pale grey leotard, emerges a figure which moves by curving in a U shape, grasping ankles, pulling, raising arms, stepping forward, U bending with straight legs until hands are flat on floor, grasping ankles, pulling. At the downward bend, the glinting hair cascades from the nape of the neck and the voice says, without strain, 'One and two and three' as the hands pull the ankles. On the hard chairs in the grey light seeping through inadequate blackout the adolescents suck in breath, gasp at the figure-revealing leotard, prepare their cliché response of the wolf whistle or hoot of derision. But the man in the grey suit is as stunned as they at the apparition. He looks with incredulity at this female shape, looks at the audience to make sure that they, too, are really seeing it, gathers their incredulity and unease into himself and channels it into a question. 'What are you doing?'

The figure comes upright. A cool voice explains, 'I'm warming up. For the performance, you know. What I am doing strengthens thighs and ankles and stretches tendons.'

The man in grey tries to absorb this information, looks at the audience over the top of his newspaper for assistance, shrugs at the incomprehensible nature of the experience and returns to his reading.

From another angle of the grey drapes appears a male figure, also in clinging grey leotard. This figure has hands on hips and is swinging first one straight leg, then the other, in a loose-hipped arc that carries the bare foot above shoulder level. This is too much. The audience's pent up embarrassment breaks in a wave of bewildered derision. The gowned staff, restless as crows, rise in an agitated flurry round the sides. But worse has happened to the man in the grey suit. The swinging leg has contacted the outstretched pages of the *Police Gazette*. His shelter from this bizarre world is crumpled and breached. He leaps to his feet, looks for sympathy to the audience, raises his eyebrows in collusion with them to show that he, too, is staggered by events, that he and they are together in a mad world. The quality of the laughter changes. Derision gives way to enjoyment. This is farce, and it is all right to laugh at the clinging leotards, at a bare-foot man who is of all perverse things, a dancer. The man in grey has channelled their sense of the absurd by sharing it with them. He has become their spokesman. So they listen when he asks, 'What's going on?'

The dancer replies, 'Out of my way, man. Can't you see what I'm doing. I'm warming up. This exercise is to mobilise the legs and hips'. His voice is mid-Western, the voice of the side-kick of the Virginian, of the hand at the Ponderosa ranch. The adolescents know that voice, that it comes from a man's world of laconic heroes. They are curious now, ready to quieten, to attend. With a rustle the crows subside, the danger past.

The performance has begun.

How I came to be sitting in that school hall, adrenaline rising in anticipatory tension, empathising with performers, feeling the stir of adolescent unease and excitement, the apprehension of staff, and sharing the wave of relaxed pleasure when, once again, the opening 'worked', dates back to October, 1973. But the sequence of events which ultimately led to that performance started in 1969 when a national ballet company was established in Scotland with headquarters in Glasgow. Although the company worked within the tradition of classical ballet the Board of Governors showed sufficient openness and flexibility to appoint in 1971 as Associate Director, Stuart Hopps, who was trained in the different idiom of modern dance. His remit was to forge links between the company and other artists working in Scotland and to build contacts with indiginous audiences, particularly young people, so that the still new company could strike roots. A series of master classes and workshops held in schools, colleges and universities culminated in 1972 in a three week tour directed by the visiting American choreographer Remy Charlip. The purpose of the programme was to offer a range of experimental movement experiences which would provide insights into choreography and dance techniques, and would enable audiences to participate in these creative processes. The response to this pilot experiment was sufficiently positive to justify further developments. It was decided that instead of borrowing classically trained dancers from the main company Stuart Hopps should recruit a group of modern dancers to form a second company, with the title *Movable Workshop*. These dancers would be interested not only in performing but in pioneering the workshop/teaching approach. Their repertoire, though designed to illumine the process of dancing, would include a range of finished items for presentation to public audiences, so that the educational work would be enriched by the standards of the professional theatre. By October, 1973, the company was in being and had a sequence of engagements already booked. Its first appearance was to be in a joint production with the Traverse Theatre, Edinburgh, of a new play by C. P. Taylor, *Columba*.

This was to be followed in January by a ten week tour of schools, colleges and universities in Scotland, culminating on April 6th with a performance at the Pitlochry Spring Festival.

I have explained the genesis of the performance I witnessed. My presence as researcher at this and many others arose from initiatives taken by the Social Aspects Department of Dunfermline College of Physical Education which funded the enquiry. This new department has as its concern the application of theoretical insights from sociology and social psychology to the field of human movement studies. The then head of department, Jean Carroll, was aware that although a considerable literature existed on the social psychology and micro-sociology of groups, very little of this related to sport, games and dance.[1] Stuart Hopps visited the college at the point when this deficiency in the literature became apparent. He was in the process of forming a group. The value of a research enquiry which would monitor the formation, development and disbanding of such a group was immediately apparent. Stuart expressed initial interest and approaches were made to the governors of the ballet company and to the college authorities, both of whom gave their approval. At that point I was invited to undertake the enquiry.

One attraction of the project for me was that it constituted research in the field setting. Though laboratory studies have provided some useful insights, the artificial segregation and limitation of variables which constitute their strength are also the source of a fundamental weakness, namely, the questionable validity of any transference of findings from this purified but potent atmosphere into the dense complexities of real life situations. My previous research in teacher education conducted from 1965 onwards had involved me in field situations and my research preference is for this setting. Moreover, since the task of *Movable Workshop* encompassed a teaching element in schools and colleges this provided a certain overlap with my earlier studies. The group members were, however, performers with a fundamental concern for

[1] For an overview of studies on small groups in sport see: Loy, W. and Kenyon, S, *Sport, Culture & Society*. New York: Macmillan, 1969.

dance as an art form and therefore they made possible a new and stimulating area of enquiry. The context of the study encompassed the, for me, unfamiliar environment of rehearsal rooms, dressing rooms, touring hotels and theatres; when it took in the familiar one of schools and colleges it was refreshingly differentiated by being within the Scottish system. Group dynamics, though implicit in the classroom and college situations I had previously researched, had not been the specific focus. Now I had the opportunity of exploring the life history of a group from its inception to its disbanding.

The fundamental importance of the concept of 'the group' lies in its acknowledgment that the individual operates in a social context which defines, modifies and intensifies whatever is recognised as his individuality:

> The self, as that which can be an object to itself, is essentially a social structure and it arises in social experience . . .
>
> It is the social process itself that is responsible for the appearance of the self; it is not there as a self apart from this type of experience . . .
>
> Only in so far as he (the human individual) takes the attitudes of the organised social group to which he belongs towards the organised co-operative social activity or set of such activities in which that group as such is engaged, does he develop a complete self or possess the sort of complete self he has developed. (Mead, 1934, pp. 140, 142, 155.)

If we are to deepen our understanding not only of human society but of the individual human being in all his unique manifestations then we must study the group.

There is, however, considerable conceptual confusion as to what constitutes a group since the term has achieved no standard meaning and has been used to designate any kind of human aggregate from subjects arbitrarily brought together in laboratory situations, individuals enacting a common role e.g. students, soldiers, factory workers,—to cohesive organisations of members from a family to a street gang to a tribe. In ordinary common sense usage the word 'group' when applied to humans indicates a recognition that something is interlinking people across individual differences. Lewin (1948, p. 184) has specified that 'something' as a process rather than a set of similar characteristics:

> A group is best defined as a dynamic whole based on interdependence rather than similarity.

This idea of interdependence has been amplified by Deutsch (1949, p. 150):

> A sociological group exists (has unity) to the extent that the individuals comprising it are pursuing promotively inter-dependent goals.

> A psychological group exists (has unity) to the extent that the individuals composing it perceive themselves as pursuing promotively interdependent goals.

It will be apparent that 'group' in the Meadian sense involves this dynamic interdependence and that the study of group processes spans, or falls between, the disciplines of both psychology and sociology. As Bales and his co-workers have asserted:

> . . . this field of research does not 'belong' to any one of the recognised social sciences alone. It is the common property of all. (Hare *et al*, 1955, p. 6)

Groups as the basic unit of social structure and as the environment by means of which we become aware of our humanity have been a frequent topic for description and reflection by historians, biographers, philosophers and novelists. Only at the end of the nineteenth century, however, when the developing social sciences made feasible the self-conscious examination of human and social phenomena were the characteristics of groups *per se* specifically examined. The controversy of the twenties on the 'reality' or otherwise of the 'group mind' shows the acute difficulty which an empirical psychology based on analogies with the natural sciences experienced in dealing with the phenomenon of groups as anything other than a collection of individuals. Allport's (1924, p. 4) assertion that only individuals are 'real'—'there is no psychology of groups which is not essentially and entirely a psychology of individuals'—did not mean, however, the abandoning of research on groups but a move from speculation into empirical investigation. Experiment in this developing field achieved its most striking results in the thirties with the publication of Moreno's (1934) *Who shall survive?*, a brilliant title ensuring maximum impact for his development of the 'sociogram', and with Lewin, Lippit and White's (1939) classic study of the effect of different styles of leadership on group atmosphere and achievement. This research generated wide interest because it suggested that miniature social and political systems could be set up in the laboratory, and the findings extrapolated to society at large. Industry, the professions and the state, all of which had a vested interest in knowledge for the preservation of the status quo, were anxious to fund such potentially useful enquiries. Thus Lewin, whose work was dedicated to advancing the construction of a general theory of groups, was enabled to set up a Research Centre for Group Dynamics at Massachusetts Institute of Technology because of an optimistic expectation by industrialists, army chiefs and politicians, as well as social workers, educationalists and doctors, that such research might solve the painful practical problems of the shop floor, the barrack room, the classroom, board room and hospital ward. The new field produced a plethora of studies characterised by meticulous rigour of design, ingenuity of experimental methodology and triviality of findings. Cartwright and Zander (1960, pp. 29, 62) surveying the field in 1960 can still strike a note of vigorous optimism:

Group dynamics may be identified by its reliance upon empirical research for obtaining data of theoretical significance, its emphasis in research and theory upon the dynamic aspects of group life, its broad relevance to all the social sciences, and the potential applicability of its findings to the improvement of social practice . . .

Group dynamics is a relatively young field and it displays the characteristics of youth. It is experiencing rapid growth and seeking a sense of identity.

By the mid sixties, disenchantment had set in. McGrath and Altman (1966, p. 79) preface their bibliography of 2692 items with the weary statement that:

> . . . the current times . . . seem to have a certain air of intellectual staleness, which contrasts with the intellectual excitement of the Lewinian era . . .

Disenchantment arose from a satiety of studies which were tailored to the requirements of the academic career structure: mass-produced, well designed, impeccable in implementation and inane in basic assumptions. Fundamental questioning of the positivist approach by both social psychologists and sociologists, and soul searching as to their role in relation to society, led to an unease about much of the work on groups which had been particularly associated with empiricism and with offering insights to the Establishment.

The study of groups has never, however, been restricted to one particular methodology or theoretical stance. While Lewin, Lippit and White (1939) were setting up their laboratory social systems, Whyte (1943) was studying gangs in the natural setting. While individuals in separate cubicles were communicating electronically, face-to-face groups derived from the psycho-analytic tradition were struggling to establish therapeutic settings in which problems of alcoholism and neurosis, or, less dramatically, of leadership and co-operation, could be explored.[2] Nor need the study of groups

---

[2] See for instances of these varied approaches, Whyte, W. F., *Street Corner Society,* Chicago: University Press, 1943. Shaw, Marvin, E., Communication Networks. In P. B. Smith (Ed) *Group Processes.* Harmondsworth: Penguin, 1970. Freud, S. Group Psychology and the Analysis of the Ego, *The Complete Psychological Works.* New York: Hogarth, 1953-64. For the group therapy approach in the United Kingdom, see: Bion, W. R., *Experience in Groups,* London: Tavistock, 1961, and a range of publications from the Tavistock Institute of Human Relations, (London).

be exploited as a means of rendering humans amenable to particular social systems and able to tolerate their strains. The group is the necessary unit of innovation and change. Anthropologists, whose discipline ensures a focus on the group, are well aware of its innovatory potential as well as conserving function. Thus Margaret Mead, writing in the sixties, asserts that the unit of micro-revolution is not the person alone, but rather the gifted person and the small group surrounding him, and sees the significant unit of evolutionary innovation as a small group of a high degree of centrality. McFeat (1974, p. 189) developing this theme suggests:

> We must know how information and ultimately group cultures can be so ordered and so specifically self-managed as to make continuing innovations possible in the field of power relations. We cannot predict innovations, but we should be able to devise conditions that encourage them.

It is therefore perfectly possible to approach the study of small groups with no sense of staleness but rather the conviction that within this dynamic unit is humanity's individuality and solidarity, permanence and potential for growth. So I took up with enthusiasm the chance to study over a five month period what was essentially a highly mobile work force involved in innovatory activity. I believed such an enquiry would have relevance beyond the study of human movement and would provide insights into general group processes and, through these, into a wide range of human concerns.

The foregoing statement implies preconceptions about the research, the foreseeing of certain potentialities offered by this particular enquiry. Without some preconceptions it would be impossible for a researcher to feel interest in an area selected for investigation. It is important, however, to be aware of these anticipations in order to minimise the imposition of externally imposed meanings and categorisations. Having acknowledged my expectations I was better able to approach the business of selecting techniques for data collection with an awareness of the inherent dangers of imposing spurious order and rationality. I intended that the research techniques should respect the insights and integrity of the individuals comprising *Movable Workshop,* and should reflect the meaning of the group experience as they perceived it.

The collection of data in the field is invariably subject to practical constraints. The dancers had come together not for self improvement as a therapy group, not to provide me with research material as a laboratory group, but to carry out a professional job. This had priority over any of my concerns. Moreover, the job entailed work at very high pressure, much of it in the public eye. Immediate impact had to be made on unfamiliar audiences and institutions: the expenditure of physical and psychic energy was at a higher pitch of intensity than is customary in a long-term professional situation. Obviously research techniques would need to be unobtrusive, flexible and in no way damaging to members' ability to carry out their task. Anything akin to 'Garfinkling',[3] that is, the disruption of expectations by manipulating accepted settings, was out.

Practical considerations were one factor in the choice of techniques: the other was, of course, the theoretical stance. There is no need to argue here the limitations of the positivist approach based on a simplistic view of what constitutes 'scientific method'. The subjective element in scientific ways of knowing has been impressively expounded by Polanyi (1958); the built-in assumptions behind so called objective data-gathering have been grittily exposed by Cicourel (1964) and the ethnomethodologists. The inadequacy of the behaviourist view of man is becoming an accepted commonplace. While approving of Wright Mills' maxim: 'Let every man be his own methodologist, let every man be his own theorist', and ready to exploit any technique likely to yield

[3] To illumine the systematic character of everyday social life Garfinkel (1967) advocates the *disruption* of expectations by the experimenter refusing to conform to one or more of the physical or verbal features of social interaction. Thus, in one experiment, he induced students to act for one hour with their own families as if they were boarders in the house.

valid evidence, I nevertheless was most in sympathy with a phenomenological approach. As Merleau-Ponty, (1974, p. 241), the existentialist phenomenologist has strikingly expressed it:

> If we actually reflect on our situation we will find that the subject, thus situated in the world and submitting to its influences, is at the same time he who thinks the world.

A spelling out of the implications of this philosophical stance is offered in relation to sociology by Filmer et al (1972) in *New Directions in Sociological Theory,* and in relation to social psychology by Harré and Secord (1972) *The Explanation of Social Behaviour.* In terms of my particular project, my concern was with what was perceived and constructed as reality by the various members of *Movable Workshop,* with the way in which they *thought* their world. I could, of course, observe them in a range of situations, but observations, no matter how disciplined or acute, can only record behaviour. This is a source of their simplifying strength, and much of their attraction to psychologists has lain in their apparent objectivity—though any system of observation operates through categories which are themselves subjectively arrived at. Observations, however, leave out the crucial element of 'intention'. Behaviours are only the outer actions of humans endowed with plans, with capacities for reflection and the attribution of meaning, with the unique gift, through language, of monitoring their own self monitoring. If I depended on observation only, I could miss the inner meaning of outward action. So not only for occasions when I was absent but also for occasions when I was present, I needed members' versions of reality:

> The social world is a subject and not an object world. It does not constitute a reality sui generis divorced from the human beings who constitute its membership. Rather, the social world is the existential product of human activity and is sustained and changed by such activity. (Walsh, 1972, p. 18)

Insights into the social world of *Movable Workshop* could never, therefore, come solely from observation. They could only arise from versions of that reality transmitted to me by members through the uniquely human tool of language. An essential research technique would therefore be the collection of spoken accounts.

My decision that the bulk of data should take the form of members' accounts is in line with the position outlined by Harré and Secord (1972). Far from being 'unscientific' such a phenomenological approach is the only one which recognises that human beings are distinguished by the ability to structure and reflect on their behaviour through language. Anyone adopting the view that 'we should treat people, for scientific purposes, *as if they were human beings'* must accept the consequence:

> In order to be able to treat people as if they were human beings it must be possible to accept their commentaries upon their actions as authentic, though revisable, reports of phenomena, subject to empirical criticism.

Of course individuals misinterpret situations, even lie. The balance is to be found in acceptance of the authentic nature of accounts with the proviso that it is legitimate to subject these to revision in the light of further evidence:

> Anyone can, in principle, give an authoritative report on whether an organism is proceeding or not, whether it is grinning or not, but only that organism itself can give an authoritative report on whether it has been watching what it was doing, feeling really happy and so on. So it seems as if one of the criteria is public and the other private. Satisfaction of the private criterion cannot be checked by any other person, but the use of public criterion is open to scrutiny by all qualified observers. Many psychologists fell into the trap of thinking that they need consider only the public criterion and use its satisfaction as the basis of the attribution of psychologically relevant predicates to people.
>
> The worry about the subjectivity and unreliability of the private criterion which led to this mistake can be put to rest

quite easily. Access and authority are two quite different concepts. It may well be that a man is the best authority as to what he is feeling and how he is proceeding, but he is not the only one with access to information of this sort. There are always some situations for any state-of-mind predicate where others have some degree of access to that state of mind even in another person . . . It nevertheless remains true that a person is the best authority as to his own states of mind, feelings and the like. Now this privilege is not absolute. What we take it to amount to is that in cases of dispute, if we wish to maintain the outside observer's point of view over against that of the person himself and his avowals then a *special case has to be made out*. (Harré & Secord, 1972, p. 122).

So the core technique would be the collection of accounts through informal interview and discussion. Such an approach, while theoretically satisfying, had the practical advantage of flexibility and unobtrusiveness. Discussions could be held with individuals, pairs, trios etc as circumstances allowed; they could be taped or written up immediately afterwards, they could be slotted into erratic time schedules. Every individual account could be cross checked by reference to other members' versions or to my own, and my own account could be cross checked back to those of other individuals. Observation could be utilised to supplement spoken statements, to provide additional evidence which could check the spoken word or be itself checked by it. Such observations would be written up immediately after the events observed. My descriptions of physical settings, though carrying strong implications because language is emotive, could have their implications checked by reference to the accounts of other participants. The collection of more formal factual material would supply a context for the accounts.

The study which follows differs in both content and tone from conventional enquiries conducted in the positivist mode. Its utilisation of the direct speech of participants, its frankness in acknowledging not only the presence of the researcher but the interaction between researcher and those being researched, is a deliberate pursuit of scientific appropriateness, which essentially depends on the methodology and presentation being suited to the nature of that which is being investigated.[4] Spurious depersonalisation has therefore been shunned. That which is being investigated is human interaction in a social context, and it is no less an authority than Weber (1964, p. 103) who reminds us:

> In the case of social collectivities, precisely as distinguished from organisms, we are in a position to go beyond merely demonstrating functional relationships and uniformities. We can accomplish something which is never attainable in the natural sciences, namely the subjective understanding of the action of the component individuals.

What follows presents a version of the social world of *Movable Workshop,* October '73–April '74. It is a version based on the most scientific evidence available, namely, the accounts of reality given in their own words by members. It differs from descriptive documentary in that every individual statement utilised has been rigorously cross-checked with statements from other individuals involved in the social action, and the researcher's own observations and interpretations have been cross-checked by reference to participants' versions of reality. Moreover, rigour of presentation arises from the researcher's attempts to place these accounts in illuminating relationship with theoretical insights drawn from the social science disciplines. In this way the individual statement ceases to be an idiosyncratic personal utterance and becomes an element in a cluster of evidence from which more generalised deductions about human interaction can be ventured. Any concept of 'absolute truth', however, is inappropriate to the social world, in that all accounts are revisable. Nevertheless, the one which follows is as authentic as an awareness of my own subjectivity can make it.

[4] For a comprehensive discussion of the methodology see Cope, E. Some Methodological issues arising from the study of a dance group in *Journal of Psycho-Social Aspects,* No. 3, Dunfermline College of Physical Education, Edinburgh, 1976.

2

INITIAL ENCOUNTERS: WHO BELONGS?

Recruitment and Membership

To focus research on a group presupposes that the group exists. I had made this obvious assumption when I agreed to undertake the present study. Had I been investigating an informal grouping I might have found that the object of enquiry disintegrated on closer examination into unrelated individuals, and that the group I was supposedly studying was a mere reification. In the case of *Movable Workshop*, however, the group as a concept had a tangible existence before it possessed individual members. Posters advertising Scottish Ballet's *Movable Workshop* were plastered on hoardings in Glasgow and Edinburgh in the summer of '73. A production was scheduled for the Traverse Theatre in December. A range of schools, colleges and universities had booked appearances from January to April '74. There was no doubting the tangible reality of a group which generated such concrete factual evidence of its existence. I had documentary proof of the actuality of my research topic.

But of course a concept may be generated and documented without being implemented. Party manifestos, blueprints, even performance schedules may project fantasies. *Movable Workshop* depended on human members to activate the programme established for it. Conditions of membership therefore became one of the initial and continuing foci of the research.

For a group to be discernable it must have boundaries: otherwise it is part of a flux or undifferentiated aggregate of humans. Parsons *et al* (1951, p. 192) have given characteristically weighty expression to this self-evident fact:

> The concept of a boundary is of crucial significance in the definition of a collectivity. The boundary of a collectivity is that criterion whereby some persons are included as members and others are excluded as non-members. The inclusion or exclusion of a person depends on whether or not he has a membership role in the collectivity. Thus all persons who have such roles are members; they are within the boundary.

The interesting question in relation to any group is obviously not 'Shall there be members?' but 'What constitutes membership?' 'How is the boundary established?' 'By what means are some people included and some excluded?' 'How do in-groupers recognise each other?' This theme of membership may seem a straightforward one, tangible and easy to grasp compared with the subtleties of within-group relationships. In fact it is far from simple. Membership, except in inert and virtually moribund groups, is not a stable state. Withdrawal or expulsion is always a lurking possibility, expansion to accommodate newcomers a necessary potential. Any dynamic group will have to deal with problems of admission and rejection, and these can never be solved on a once and for all basis. The drawing of a boundary is a technique for rendering the group recognisable: it is also a protection for indwellers and a barrier for those outside. Strategies for crossing the boundary are a fascinating topic for study. With some groups they can be informal, tentative, only partially articulated. With others they can be ritualised to a high degree until they become virtually *rite de passage*. Whatever form they take, they are a highly significant indication of the nature of a given group and its state of activation. In spite of this they have been subjected to little enquiry.[1] Recruitment has, of course, long been a topic of sociological study, and statistical surveys in terms of class membership have been made of recruits to élite or professional groups.[2] The role of selection as a means of social control has been emphasised by Etzioni (1964) in *Modern Organizations*. But 'boundary crossing strategies' in specific case contexts have been little examined, though Trist *et al* (1970 p. 50-51) stress their importance in relation to work groups in industrial settings:

> The psychological climate of a group and the kinds of relationship it has with other groups involved in completing the same primary task is to a considerable degree determined by the way the groups are built up. It is important to determine the route through which men achieve membership of particular groups, the permanency of membership and the route by which men leave.

Whereas informal social groupings may depend solely on semi-articulated class, income and shared interest criteria of membership, professional and work groups obviously require appropriate skills, qualifications and experience. These latter groups may utilise the formal organisational method of an interview or audition as part of the selection process. Such devices enable a subjective assessment of personality to be made, while paradoxically ensuring that acceptance appears more objective and rejection more impersonal. In a situation where there is balanced recruitment from a standardised field, formal methods may be used exclusively. In many

---

[1] Aronson and Mills (1960) have demonstrated in the laboratory situation that severity of initiation intensifies liking for the group. Little work has been done in the field situation, however, to examine the processes by means of which individuals are inducted into groups.

[2] See, for instance, R. K. Kelsall's *Higher Civil Servants in Britain*, London: Routledge & Kegan Paul, 1955, or for an overview, T. B. Bottomore *Elites and Society*, New York: C. A. Watts, 1964.

situations, however, formal selection processes are modified, either because too many appropriately qualified persons are clamouring for membership of exclusive groups, or, alternatively, because there is no clearly defined field of recruitment and potential members have to be sighted and invited across the boundary.

What was the recruitment position in relation to *Movable Workshop?* As a professional company it had at its disposal a formal means of admission, namely, the audition. As a modern dance company, however, it could call on no standardised form of qualification. Moreover, the supply of professionals, particularly men, skilled in modern dance techniques to the level of theatrical performance is strictly limited in this country. Whereas in the U.S.A. there are numerous degree courses in modern dance and a range of professional companies offering training and experience, in the U.K. at the time of writing degrees are only just being initiated, training, other than in association with teacher training, is available only at the London School of Contemporary Dance, and companies of professional standing are only beginning to emerge. To complicate recruitment problems, the goals of *Movable Workshop* required that members should be not only skilled performers but competent teachers, able to handle children and students in workshop situations. Given the duality of these requirements and the dearth of adequately experienced recruits it was hardly likely that the fleshing of *Movable Workshop* with members would proceed by formal channels and without complications.

When I first visited Glasgow on October 31st 1973, to start the research, the company already comprised five people: Stuart Hopps, instigator and founder member, three dancers and one musician.

Lynda Colston and Fionna McPhee, the two women dancers, had both been students at Dartington College of Arts from 1969-72. After receiving the Specialist Teachers' Diploma of Dance and Drama they had gone for a year's further training in Holland to the Rotterdam Dansacademie. Stuart Hopps had been at Dartington from 1970–71 as 'artist in residence' where he had been tutor to both girls. He visited the Dansacademie during their training year and checked on progress. In August he invited Lynda to join the group. Then in October he contacted Fionna and offered her a position. Originally this was principally to teach, but this plan was modified by the course of events and Fionna shared fully in the performances.

Gary Cobb, the male dancer, was a young American who had studied dance at the Universities of Maryland and New Mexico. Before completing his degree course he came over to the Edinburgh Festival with the New Mountain Dance Company, a small group with whom he had been dancing intermittently for some time. In Edinburgh he was involved in some Fringe dance activities, encountered Stuart Hopps, collaborated with him in a number of workshops and was invited to join the company.

Bob Stuckey, the twenty-nine year old musician, had behind him varied experience, including accompanying dancers at The Place, headquarters of the Contemporary Dance Company. For the last two years he had studied music at Glasgow University and in 1973 composed the music for a student production. This was seen by Stuart Hopps, who subsequently invited him to join *Movable Workshop*.

Thus all the group members I first met had been acquired by the process of 'sighting and inviting'. The formal procedures of auditioning had been unnecessary since alternative opportunities for assessing skills had been available.

Interestingly enough, however, two dancers had been recruited by audition and had already left before my arrival. These were a man and woman dancer straight from an established ballet school. Though the school offered a basically classical training, Stuart had felt that its ethos was sufficiently innovatory and flexible for the pair to fit in. I was not, of course, concerned with attempting to trace 'the facts' of their three weeks' experience prior to their withdrawal, but instead with discovering the effect of this on the remaining members, and the manner in which they accounted for what had happened. In view of the membership problems which the group had already encountered, I was delighted that my first afternoon session with the company, on October 31st, should involve the auditioning of potential newcomers.

My observations of this session, written up immediately after the event, were based on first impressions before I knew any of the group as individuals. Stuart I had met for the first time at lunch, and I returned with him to the rehearsal studio at the Opera Centre. After a brief introduction to the dancers I was given a chair in front of the mirrored wall and the session began. I was very conscious that as yet I had no knowledge as to whether individual dancers would be willing to participate in the research. An irony of this auditioning session was that I, too, had to prove myself acceptable to the company.

The two potential new dancers were an American, David Johnson, and a Canadian, Larry MacKinnon. (David Johnson is a fictitious name given to preserve anonymity since this dancer was not present at the agreement to participate in the research. All other members are referred to by their actual names.) Both had had previous dance experience in their own countries with small professional companies and both had done further training at The Place. Larry had then dropped out from dancing for eight months and had worked in a vegetarian restaurant. Then, wishing to get back on to form, he had resumed training at the Dance Centre taking ballet classes. He heard of Stuart's project from a Glasgow friend, phoned him, and Stuart came to London to see him do a class. In the same class was the American, David, who was still training at The Place. Stuart invited both to Glasgow and, to guard against over-hasty acceptance and the possibility of subsequent resignations, he arranged for them to spend several days with the Company.

The piece being rehearsed was *Zodiac,* choreographed by the musician, Bob Stuckey, to his own score of taped electronic sounds supplemented by zither chords. As musician he sat cross-legged at the far side of the room, striking complex counter rhythms from the zither across his knees: as choreographer he rose to his feet to give further directions and occasionally demonstrated. Fionna, Lynda, Gary and Stuart danced as the team drawing the Sun God's chariot across the sky. Bob had evolved the broad movements but details had still to be worked out and the dancers were trying out various possibilities. Stuart was performing merely as fill-in for the absent male dancer. He was very quick at responding to suggestion and providing new movements of a more exaggerated kind to suggest the struggle and exhaustion of the pulling group. I noticed that while the other dancers remained in role or stood passive, he slipped in and out of role frequently, one minute performing, the next observing, appraising and commenting. None of this was done subversively to diminish Bob's authority as choreographer, since he worked strenuously with the others to fill out the initial ideas. I had a feeling, however, that this slipping from role carried a message both to me and to the other newcomers. It was a reminder that while he was willing to perform, his primary professional task was not that of the dancer. It demonstrated to us his expertise, showing us inventiveness in devising movements, speed in assuming a role, while at the same time informing us that his true task was that of overall director.

David took the dominant part of the Sun God, with Larry as attendant Mercury, circling close. David had a striking physical appearance—a shock of dark hair, a profile of eighteenth century hauteur, and a wide and expressive movement range, brilliant to the brink of the bizarre. Larry was a softer and more immediately attractive dancer, fluid, technically accomplished, less assertive but with plenty of projection. Both on probation, they were singled out by their roles, while the rest of the dancers laboured and writhed, pulling the chariot. The Sun God had slow, stylised movements, his arm swung in a great arc, wielding an imaginary whip: Mercury circled him closely, in the pull of his orbit. Their assigned parts isolated them from the existing group, which laboured as a team. Rationally this casting was justified since it provided them with a test piece suited to their physical gifts. Its effect was to place them in dominant roles over the rest of the dancers. I was strongly conscious of an assurance that could have arisen from characterisation but which seemed to have more than artistic origins.

Afterwards Stuart rehearsed a dance which he had choreographed for the original group, particularly for the two classically trained ballet dancers. *Handelabra* was a light-hearted pastiche, a pseudo-classical partner dance requiring a polished deftness of performance if it was to work. Since it had deliberate balletic characteristics it was scarcely likely to appeal to newcomers from the Place. Stuart explained—almost semi-apologetically—that it had been devised for the dancers who had left. The explanation seemed to be as much for David and Larry as for me. Lynda was familiar with the part, but Gary and Fionna struggled to fill the void left by the missing couple. The ethos of the dance, coupled with their insecurity in newly assumed parts, constituted a powerful reminder of the ones who had gone. Fionna broke down frequently; every time she forgot, she signalled she was out of role by a gesture of rubbing her nose and staring wide-eyed at Stuart, disarming criticism. Gary danced uncertainly, his movements embarrassed and self conscious rather than deft. David and Larry swathed themselves in the grotesque medley of woollen socks, old sweaters and plastic sweat suits which I discovered were normal wear in rehearsals and sat on the floor at the side. Silent watchers, previously dominant, they now formed a powerful pair. David began to smoke; after a moment Larry leaned across and lit up a cigarette from David's. After watching a short time, they broke off to exercise at the side, as if total concentration on this effort was unnecessary. I felt that a strong sense of unease was being generated, and that in complete reversal of all my expectations it was the existing group that was vulnerable and uncertain and those being auditioned who were dominant, even threatening.

During the tea break I was put through my own audition, or rather interview by the dancers. Naturally some searching questions were asked about the amount of their time I would take, the demands the research would make on the group, whether I thought an investigation of group dynamics would prove tolerable and what kind of research report I had in mind. During this discussion Stuart called David out to another room, obviously to resolve some issue and, perhaps, to leave the company dancers free to reach their own decision. Larry was left behind, however, and was incorporated into the questioning. I answered as frankly as I could: that I would fit the demands of the research around their priorities; that obviously an investigation of a developing group could be threatening and they might indeed find that they could not tolerate it, but the intention was to use the data constructively; that as yet I could not anticipate the precise kind of research report but that all group members would see the draft. I felt that trust could only be engendered by open acknowledgment of their fears and my own uncertainties. For as Jourard (1971, p. 17) has pointed out in *The Transparent Self*:

> Man is master of the mendacious arts. If this is true and if students of human experience and behaviour are interested in learning something about man, then the *relationship between the person being studied and the one studying him is called into question*. If you want to study me and I don't know you or trust you, I'll kick you out, or I'll lie to you.

I was not kicked out: or, to express it more formally, the dancers agreed to collaborate. It seemed of some significance that Larry should have joined in this agreement; as if Stuart's action in withdrawing David had split the strong partnership I had been conscious of during the afternoon, leaving Larry to be incorporated in the group.

I left after securing this agreement and arranging to revisit in a week's time, when I would follow an observation session with an evening of tape recordings. I needed to check my initial impressions with individual accounts and see how closely, if at all, they related to the reality perceived and constructed by the dancers.

The following Wednesday I returned to Glasgow. I was not surprised to find that of the two dancers, Larry had been retained, the official explanation being that there would have been difficulties about a work permit for David. The pseudoclassical piece, *Handelabra,* was again being rehearsed. Lynda, competent in her role, was dancing with crisp assurance; Fionna and Gary, now that Fionna had memorised the actual choreography, were achieving some of pastiche elegance which the frivolity of the piece demanded; Larry, technically accomplished, was picking up his part rapidly. The atmosphere was quite different from the anxiety and tension of the previous week. Instead of expressions of dismay and self disgust, there were smiles and laughter when an effect became ludicrous through misjudgment. Stuart showed no sign of irritation when the rhythm was lost or a sequence forgotten. He would demonstrate—re-instruct—say mildly, 'Let's try it again'. The five worked strenuously but without strain.

At tea break the atmosphere seemed equally relaxed. I was conscious that in the evening we were to have the first taped interviews but no-one seemed particularly concerned. There were one or two joking references to the fact that I was carrying the tape-recorder—'Better watch out' 'Is it on yet?' 'You'll be able to blackmail us', but the jokes did not seem to have the edge of real anxiety. I felt much more at ease myself than the week before when I, too, had been on probation. We drank tea perched uncomfortably on the broken down furniture of the small room which led from the dance studio. Lynda smoked and knitted. Stuart got up to help Fionna master a particular movement sequence they were discussing. He showed her how to curve over, to pull in abdominally and round her back as she lifted the left leg. Fionna, who had gone through years of ballet training as a child, had developed the characteristic soaring upward pull of the spine, and found this flexible, boneless curving difficult. Larry got up and demonstrated the movement. He then went over and manipulated her back in order to help her feel the necessary movement in the discs of the spine. He seemed very much at home in the group, already fully integrated. The fact that there was no strict demarcation into work and social, but that individuals moved easily from idle chatter into a highly technical demonstration of a movement point, then back again, suggested:

(1) that my presence was accepted. There was no attempt to keep the tea break 'social' for my benefit.

(2) the dancers were more strongly affected by work goals than the week before. Fionna showed no self-consciousness or resentment at this coaching *outside* the studio situation.

(3) from being outside the group the week before, Larry seemed now well integrated. He took the initiative, and offered advice to supplement Stuart's.

After tea we travelled by 'bus to Fionna's flat. I interviewed in a separate room, one person at a time, while the others came and went, organising their own sequence. As a result of a joint decision, I addressed all members by their first names and was addressed back as Edith. I have accordingly utilised first names in quotations, diagrams and references. At this stage I am selecting from these discussions only those elements which are relevant to the theme of recruitment and membership. Other elements from this first session are utilised in the themes of later chapters.[3]

What emerged very clearly from the account of the first few weeks given separately by Lynda, Fionna and Gary was the disquieting effect of the withdrawal of the two classically trained dancers. For a newly formed group of five, the loss of two members is traumatic. The survivors appeared to have dealt with this by supplying a version of motives for withdrawal which stressed the leavers' limitations and allowed the survivors to continue functioning, their goals intact. Shaken as they were by the event, this emergence of an

---

[3] The interviews were unstructured. I opened this first one by asking individuals to tell me what had happened so far. All subsequent interviews I opened by asking 'What has happened since I last saw you?' Only in playing through the taped material several times at the end of the research did the themes which form the 10 chapters emerge as *my* way of structuring the material. Themes were never mentioned to the participants nor was any discussion structured round them.

acceptable explanation was a very necessary process. The two had left because they were primarily interested in their individual performances and were out of sympathy with the workshop side:

LYNDA They just weren't interested in it at all. They could see no point in showing children dance or bringing dance to the masses. They only wanted to perform so that people would acknowledge what brilliant dancers they were.

GARY The two from the ballet school didn't really want to try anything new or really to extend themselves beyond what they already knew. I think they were very afraid, in a way.

FIONNA At Dartington it was very much working as a group, especially in drama—you give so much to people and it's always a two way thing. But I found that the two ballet trained people had a different conception of how the work would go. They were very conscious of their own individual training—their individual performance—less of making the thing work as a group.

The failure of the original group to coalesce was attributed not to personality clashes but to different backgrounds of training:

'Was there any personality conflict?'

FIONNA Not so much personality as attitude to dance or attitude to the aim we were working for. I think personality could have worked. They were used to a more authoritative approach. They were straight from school and then three years at ballet school where everything is set for you. In ballet everything is set—the technique, the choreography. Whereas in modern there's a much freer style. And I think they weren't sure perhaps of what they wanted. They were only starting as well. They were very worried about improvisations and working with different groups of people.

So the embryonic company split, according to the accounts given by the survivors, on the respectable grounds of differing training backgrounds and goals. There is no reason to doubt that these were important elements. In general terms, for a task group to work together effectively individuals must sympathise with the expressed goals, and must be able to perceive the way in which their personal contribution helps in the achievement of these goals. Members recruited from different training backgrounds will obviously have difficulty with both these requirements in the initial stages. In the field of dance these difficulties are enhanced by the fact that not only are training backgrounds divergent but, until recently, considerable waryness and suspicion has existed between exponents of the various schools. Thus ballet possesses a highly prestigious and effective technique of training on an authoritarian and hierarchical basis. Against this can be set the equally disciplined and exclusive training of the Martha Graham school. Developments by Merce Cunningham are powerfully idiosyncratic. The ethos of modern dance as influenced by educational ideas, particularly Rudolph Laban's, is more exploratory, more tentative, less focused on highly disciplined performance and more on personal and group participation in a—hopefully—creative process.[4] From fear of contamination, protagonists of the various schools of dance have tended to be partisan. Only recently has an ecumenical movement gained ground. Now attempts are being made to evolve links, but the products of the varied existing methods of training inevitably manifest different levels of skill, different kinds of technical expertise, different value judgments and different goals. Where such divergencies exist within a group, then it is difficult to avoid splitting.

Other elements which intensified the problems can be deduced from the evidence. After the explicitness of ballet performance, the job requirements were both vague and threatening. In such a situation very strong support would

---

[4] For insight into this approach see Laban, Rudolph, *Modern Educational Dance,* London: MacDonald & Evans, 1948, and Russell, Joan, *Modern Dance in Education,* London: MacDonald & Evans, 1958.

have been needed during the transitional period. Instead the two ballet trained dancers would find that a within-group group already existed. Lynda knew Stuart from her own professional training; Gary had worked with him during the Festival; Fionna, when she arrived, merely renewed the links well established at Dartington:

LYNDA I knew Stuart very well. It wasn't any problem for me to understand what he was saying or doing. Gary knew him fairly well. He'd known him all the summer and had been working with him so it was easier for him.

A network of relationships was already established. It is possible that the two newcomers may have been alienated not only by different backgrounds and goals, but by existing alliances. They may have perceived the original members as a strongly cohesive group involved in activities which were to them disturbing and threatening to the standards already inculcated and internalised. It would not be surprising, therefore, if they felt increasingly isolated and at odds.

Bob Stuckey, the musician, watched this splitting from the side lines:

I feel that I'm apart from the dancers because I can't share all their experiences and knowledge—you know—and be complaining of an aching back or a twisted muscle. I can't really think of a time when I've felt like that. They use terms I don't understand and they have priorities I don't understand. They hold certain companies in high esteem that I've only vaguely heard of. I took a back seat because the dancers had more discernment of other dancers than I had and they very quickly separated themselves from these two. Had they not done I should probably never have noticed anything about them.

The rift reached dimensions that could not be ignored:

LYNDA Stuart decided, finally, one day that this wasn't what they wanted to be doing and that they weren't happy.

He invited them to leave. After their departure, the surviving members explained the withdrawal in terms of differing backgrounds and values, not of any clashes of personality or conflicting inner alliances. Such an explanation, because it entailed reiteration of goals, performed a necessary constructive repair job.

Any newly-formed group is threatened by loss of members. There may be initial relief as dissidents withdraw and a cohesive nucleus is left, but the withdrawal is both a rejection and an attenuation.[5] The recruitment of replacements will be coloured by wariness and unease. It was this that came through in the audition session which I observed. My impressions were fully confirmed by the dancers' accounts of their feelings:

FIONNA It was very upsetting when they went because we were just beginning to think that perhaps things were going to work—just getting some pieces finished and perhaps the beginnings of our own concept of how this venture would turn out. Then suddenly half the group's gone. You find yourself wondering, 'What on earth will happen? Will we just break up or will we find people? What sort of people do we want? Will they change the group again and make it a new idea?'

GARY When they left and two new boys came—suddenly we had a new identity even though it was chancy that they might stay. And this was really interesting but I felt sort of insecure. It was as though we were on display and they were deciding whether they liked us or not. It was rather nerve racking for a while.

---

[5] For a discussion of the complex reactions of 'study group' members to a person who withdraws see Richardson, Elizabeth, *Group Study for Teachers,* London: Routledge and Kegan Paul, 1967, pp. 112-13.

LYNDA They were watching and assessing us as much as
Stuart was assessing them. It was very strange having
two strangers coming in on three people who got on
very well.

These statements not only amply validate my observations.
Lynda's 'two strangers coming in on three people' implicitly
recognises Stuart's and Bob's separation by their roles from
the actual dancers. And the dancers already have a concept of
'the group' as an emergent reality, with a developing identity
which will be derived from, but which will over-ride, their
individuality.

After the week of auditions, why was Larry selected and not
David? The official reason was that there would have been
difficulties in securing a work permit for David since he was
American and the company already employed an American
dancer in Gary. The unofficial reasons were linked with the
group's past history. The desire was to avoid further strain
and splitting. David's personality was believed to be more
demanding and his priorities possibly different:

LYNDA David stayed in my flat while he was here and I just
had nothing but his problems. This was fine just for
me but it's very hard for a group to take someone
else's burden. Gary, Fionna and I have all got
problems but we keep them out of the group thing.

FIONNA I think really for David this was an alternative
situation rather than a first choice and for that reason
wasn't a very good idea. It was a substitute, a
substitute for the performances he would rather have
been involved in in London.

So the reasons for the selection of one and the rejection of the
other were being structured on a basis of the group's needs
and goals. I had certainly gained the feeling the week before,
while the probationary period was still under way, that Larry
was being incorporated and David separated off before any
public decision had been reached.

Now that Larry was a member of the company the wariness had evaporated and he was viewed with warmth and optimism:

FIONNA Larry has fitted in very quickly.
LYNDA I think Larry's getting on marvellously well.
GARY I think it will work. Larry's bringing in a lot of new ideas to the group and he's very solid technically and he's a good teacher as well—he's good.

How did Larry himself perceive the sequence of events? It was possible that though I had been correct in attributing unease and wariness to the company members, I had been wrong in feeling a counter-balancing assurance in the two probationers. Was the assurance just part of the professional 'act', masking anxiety and insecurity? It seemed not. Larry commented on his initial impressions:

Not knowing anyone it seemed like they'd all been together for a long time, but they hadn't.

Since this suggested that the existing dancers might have presented a somewhat formidable united front, I asked,

'Did you feel it might be difficult to get yourself in?'

Larry was genuinely puzzled:

I think it was I wasn't sure I wanted to. It didn't occur to me—I wasn't going with the intention of really trying to get in, because from the way Stuart explained it I would have thought there was a greater need for—I'm sounding pompous—I didn't think his problem was as much to find a fantastic dancer as to get someone who would work with the group. In fact I guess as far as professional experience I'd more really than the rest of the people.

There was no complacency of tone as Larry said this—in fact

there was the social embarrassment of someone trying to be honest when the honesty leads to self-inflating remarks. The key question for Larry quite genuinely seemed to have been not 'Will I prove acceptable during this probationary period?' but 'Do I want to take up this job?' It was not surprising, then, that the episode of the audition had been invested with such unexpected emotional tone.

In spite of Larry's rapid integration it was interesting that he made no mention of the topic which featured so frequently in the discussions of the others, namely, 'the group', that organism whose goals they had both to formulate and to serve. His expressed aspirations were for himself:

> 'What persuaded you to stay?'

LARRY I don't know. I think it was the opportunity to choreograph a piece of my own. I don't know how well I can work in situations like this. But creating pieces is creating pieces; to have it shown would be worth while.

> 'So really the kind of fulfilment you are looking for in the near future is on the choreography side?'

LARRY Definitely. And just working with a different kind of moving. I mean, I've only done Graham, which is a very definite technique on its own and Stuart teaches something very different. Again we do ballet classes each week and I've had very little of that. A lot of Graham dancers I suppose would look down on that because they get very closed on what they are doing. I'm trying to look on it as a new experience and hopefully I'll gain from it.

> 'So for the time being this seems to be meeting your own professional ambitions? Or did you put them on one side so much in the last eight months that now you are just groping—and this group happens to be available?'

LARRY It sounds horrible but I think a lot of what you said is true.

He has not yet acquired the vocabulary and orientation of the others. This could be a sign of his newness in the situation; he has not yet been socialised into their version of their goals and their own roles in relation to those goals. Or it could be a sign of a more deeply-rooted divergence.

The person ultimately responsible for allowing people across the boundary and officially recognising their membership was, of course, Stuart Hopps. There is considerable significance in the fact that he alone of the entire membership gave no explanations or justifications of the decisions taken. In his discussion with me he was concerned to place the present group in their historical context; to describe the earlier experiments and to foresee future developments. In such a context the present *Movable Workshop* was an episode; its membership a professional problem to be solved. Hiring and firing are part of a paid routine for management: selection of personnel is an important task but only one in a complex mesh of planning, decision-taking and action. For the director of a dance group, selection is particularly important because his personal prestige and the success of the programme are dependent not on any machines but on the human members of a small team. But for management even in this situation there is little point, once selection has been made, in introspecting on possible consequences. These will reveal themselves only too surely in the course of events. So the choice of Larry was not commented on at any stage in Stuart's interview. And the only reference to the early loss of members was, 'You have heard the saga of the two from the ballet-school.' This comment demonstrates a sense of solidarity with the surviving dancers—it assumes that the version of events they have supplied corresponds with his own view of the situation and that there is no need for an authoritative gloss. The lack of additional justifications and the concentration on broader issues seems a clear indication that though he saw himself as an integral member of the group, he operated in a broader professional context which diminished the significance of specific incidents. His awareness of the problems created by changes of membership caused him to exercise great caution in the second stage of recruitment—hence the procedure of newcomers spending several days with the company. Yet the main issues were not to him those of individual membership but of over-all aims, and it was to the exposition of these and his own motives and aspirations that Stuart utilised the interview. What was of such central concern to the inexperienced young dancers who had to absorb the social repercussions of choice, was to him a professional task.

If numbers were to be restored, the company still needed a further member. I was told that Peter Allan, a young dancer also from the Place. was coming up the following week to spend a few days with the group. On November 14th I went over to Glasgow to sit in on a further audition/rehearsal. Once again, the piece was *Zodiac*. This time the role of the Sun God was taken by Peter. I had a very strong sense of recurring pattern. The stylised movements, the sense of dominant and dominated, the electronic vibrations—all created the powerful atmosphere of a *rite de passage*. All interviews and auditions have their symbolism,[6] but this audition rite was given an extra dimension by the fact that the test of skill was in itself mythical in content and ritualised in movement. It was fascinating to observe how this stereotyped episode could be invested with a quite different emotional tone. The team drawing the chariot had by now fully mastered their choreographic sequences and danced with power and as-surance. Peter, as Sun God, had a height and build suited to dominance. His movements, however, lacked the vigour and idiosyncracy of David's: he sketched out the sequence, but the broad gestures lacked that assertive assurance. Larry, circling close, seemed threatening rather than supportive. The dominance was not with this Sun God but with the lesser planets, and in the centre of the ceremony was the uneasy

[6] The candidate's solitary chair, placed centrally, facing a long table formally set out with files and papers, denotes one type of interview, as does a grouping of chairs round a coffee table, denoting a probably spurious informality. The social skills involved in interviews have been described by Argyle, Michael, *The Social Psychology of Work*, Harmondsworth: Penguin, 1974, pp. 158-61, and a training film has been produced by Sidney, E., & Argyle, M., *Selection Interviewing*, London: Mantra Ltd, 1969.

probationer, performing with an earnest commitment but under strain.

As for the general mood, apart from Peter's natural anxiety there was an atmosphere of light hearted *camaraderie*, totally different from a fortnight earlier. Larry moved off claiming it was tea break time and getting an apple from among his gear at the side. There was some physical by-play as Fionna and Gary tried for the apple. Stuart asserted himself by saying, 'Let's save eating until the tea break.' It was the first time I had seen him do more than suggest or murmur or discuss. The group fell back into line amiably, Larry still grinning and very much one of the gang.

At the tea break Peter confided to me that he would very much like to be selected. He had come to dancing late in life, moving at twenty-one from a job as technician in a research laboratory to training at the Place. Even after three years he was aware that technically he had still a lot of lost time to make good. He made no attempt to disguise this, nor to hide his desire to be chosen. The other dancers were kindly and ready to be welcoming. Stuart asked them to keep Peter company that evening as he himself had to go to Edinburgh. They came in quickly with invitations, seemingly aware that Peter as an unaccompanied probationer was bound to feel a little solitary and exposed. The impression was of a secure group who could afford to be kindly.

After the tea break Larry and Fionna rehearsed a dance which Larry was choreographing, and in a separate studio Gary and Lynda worked on one of Gary's. There was a strong rapport between the individuals in each pair. A catch was bungled, and Larry claimed that the blunder was 'my fault', while Fionna accepted responsibility—each was very considerate of the other. I went into the second studio just at a point when a movement phrase fortuitously echoed the words of the song which provided the music, and an unintentionally ludicrous effect ensued. Lynda was ready to see the absurd but Gary smiled wryly, wholly in earnest and anxious to work out the sequence. Lynda immediately sobered and worked hard to help Gary realise his ideas. With these pairs strongly established, I wondered how a newcomer would manage to get himself incorporated. Stuart was evidently sensitive to the situation. On the train to Edinburgh he speculated as to whether another dancer was strictly necessary. I had a strong feeling that I had been seeing a group which had reached a comfortable stage of being able to work together without strain. As Mills (1970, p. 149) has pointed out:

1st Stage of Membership: October 1st 1973.

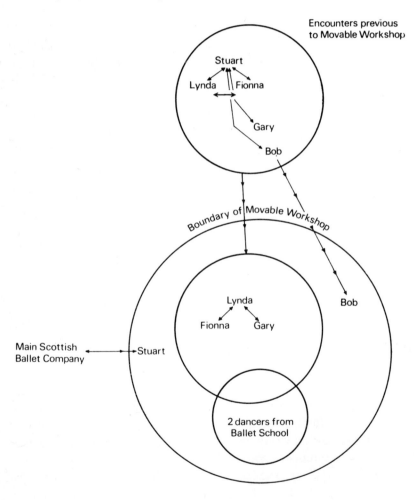

The arrival of an outsider changes the situation both for him and for the group, setting in motion reactions to the change and processes of mutual adjustment which may or may not be satisfactory in their outcome.

With stability so recently established, it would be natural if the dominant desire of members should be to maintain the group as it was, without the disruption of further change. It is perhaps of some significance that the membership situation I have outlined lasted until the New Year, a decision on Peter being tacitly deferred.

To supplement this verbal exposition I shall present the different membership stages and the inter-relationships within them by means of diagrams.

Although within the boundary of *Movable Workshop,* Stuart Hopps interacts with the main company through contacts with the Director, Peter Darrell, the Board of Governors and the Administrative staff.

Within *Movable Workshop* are two subgroups comprising the dancers. Three of these are known to Stuart outside the context of the Company. The two girls have long established links with each other. Gary and Lynda have developed a relationship with each other in work situations within the company. Bob as musician feels separated from the dancers. He also has encountered Stuart prior to the *Movable Workshop* situation. The two from the ballet school are known only in the context of the *Workshop*. They form a pair with different backgrounds, recruited by different means.

2nd Stage of Membership, October 31st

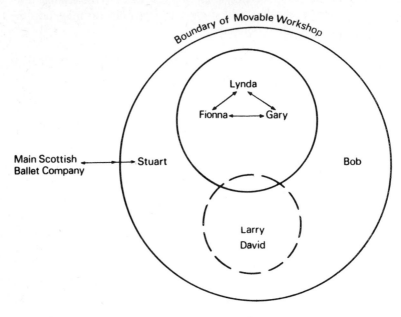

3rd Stage of Membership, November 6th.

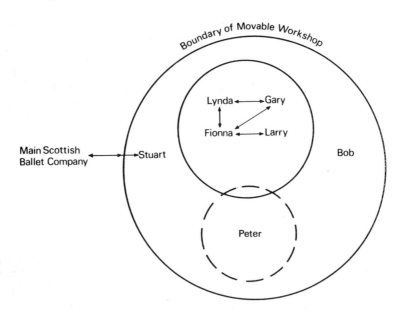

This examination of the early stages in the formation of a dance group has revealed some of the complexities of recruitment and membership. The way in which people are recruited tells us something about the nature of the group they are joining: it is moreover a significant factor in their feelings about the work situation and the organisation of which they have become members. Bob, Fionna, Lynda and Gary, by being 'sighted and invited', would feel a flattering sense of being suited to the work in hand. Those who crossed the boundary by audition would start without this initial psychological advantage. The utilisation of varied means of recruitment is an indication of the lack of standardised qualifications and the scarcity of the desired product. Informal as well as formal means are necessary in such situations. But the informal means of recruitment, with its personalised approaches, arises additionally from two other circumstances. In work of short duration and high intensity, all members must rapidly develop a *modus vivendi,* a swift rapport. A director of a dance group by the nature of his job operates in face to face situations; he will wish to recruit persons he feels he can readily work with, who will readily work with each other. Previous knowledge gained in other situations may appear more dependable than the swift display given in auditions, even auditions extended over several days. The third factor links with power and patronage. 'Sighting and inviting' results from scarcity of the desired product. To offer the invitation is, however, an act of power, involving the bestowal of patronage. In the insecurity of the world of the theatre the right to select the personal mode over the impersonal bestows power, even if fleeting. An element of personal patronage is to be expected in a highly insecure profession.

Auditions and interviews may be utilised to confirm 'sighting and inviting' or as an alternative. In the former case they may be simulation exercises where some or all participants play out their roles *as if* decisions, already taken, depended on performances. In the latter case they are genuine decision-forming and decision-taking situations. Always they are 'formal episodes' as explicated by Harré and Secord (1972, p. 171):

> A formal episode has an explicit script. Much that is clearly formal in character may be bound only by quasi-rules or conventions which could be written down but have been learnt not by reading and following the rule book, but perhaps by scrutiny of earlier performances and imitation of them and so on.

Auditions, however, differ from most interviews in that they frequently contain within their already formal structure a simulation which is totally rule bound. Thus a dancer may be required to enact a specific choreography, an actor to read a script. According to the content, the already ritualised nature of the situation may be shattered or enhanced. Thus an audition requiring an actor to simulate a burst of laughter followed by a sudden shock of pain would temporarily suspend the sense of ritual inherent in the rule bound social situation. If the actor were required to enact an episode from *Oedipus Tyranus,* however, the sense of ceremonial generated by the simulated episode would colour the social situation. Thus auditions are pseudo-competitive or genuinely competitive formal situations which provide complex layers of meaning. The two episodes I observed were invested with an additional ceremonial element by the mythical nature of the dance content, so that I perceived them as *rite de passage.* Yet social and professional performances within the rule bound script differed considerably and the meaning of episode I, attested by observation and confirmed by discussion, was very different from the meaning of episode II.

In any work groups, different training backgrounds embodying different value systems inevitably lead to difficulties in functioning. Goals may be misinterpreted or even rejected. Considerable time and skill is necessary if differences are to be worked through and used as sources of strength. Where participants have the insecurity of only just embarking on professional careers, and where time is at a premium, the most likely consequence is that the work group will split into factions. Sequence I shows this, exacerbated by the fact that the subgroups had different relationships with the leader.

The loss of members in the early stages is very damaging to morale. The experienced leader, seeing this in a broader perspective, may view it with rather more equanimity. The remaining members of the work group, after initial relief, feel a strong sense of diminution and loss. This can reach the point where the group's very survival is seen as hypothetical. New members are desired, but there is anxiety in case they too, reject the group. Anyone recruited at this stage has an advantage over a somewhat demoralised membership. He has to face initial wariness, however, and the possibility that once the barriers have been crossed and he belongs, too much renewed optimism will be invested in him.

When a group has acquired, after difficulties, members who are apparently learning to work together cohesively, it may be reluctant to face the strains inherent in incorporating newcomers. The status-quo may appear more attractive than the risks involved in further recruitment. This seemed to be the stage reached by mid-November and my reading of the situation received some confirmation by the fact that a decision on Peter was tacitly postponed. Thus *Movable Workshop* entered on the preparations for its first public engagement at the Traverse Theatre with a work force comprising six people; a director, a musician, and two pairs of dancers.

3

GROUP IDENTITY AND THE SAINT:

Conflict and Disintegration

The first public engagement for the Company was at the Traverse Theatre, December 12th, in a play, *Columba,* based on the life of the Celtic saint. The author, C. P. Taylor, had devised it as a mixed media presentation incorporating music and dance integrally with a spoken script, and so four actors and three musicians were involved with *Movable Workshop* members. The dancers moved over to Edinburgh three weeks before the opening date to start rehearsals. There was anticipatory excitement at the thought of working in Edinburgh on a production designed for public presentation.

On November 23rd I went to the theatre to watch a rehearsal. The Traverse has, of course, an exciting reputation for its experimental productions. It is housed unimpressively, however, in the upper floors of a tenement building in the old city and the physical setting is very congested. Seating is movable to allow for maximum flexibility of use of the small auditorium for theatre in the round etc. The seats consist of bulky padded levels of foam, forming tiers up which the audience must swarm to take their places. The walls are painted black. The daytime effect of the black walls and the plumped brown tiers, without the colour of a seated audience or the focus of a spot-lit stage, is stiflingly claustrophobic. In the harsh general lighting the set for the current play, still in position, looked battered and tatty, the floor space squalid.

Stuart was rehearsing a section where actors, musicians and dancers were involved in a combined sequence. The one actress moved very expressively, but the three men actors were bulky and clumsy in comparison with the dancers. They participated energetically, however, tackling the movement routine without any self-consciousness. The choreography was simplified so as not to present too many problems and they worked at it with some gusto. The dancers presented a marked contrast. Their participation was obviously half-hearted; the movements offered them no challenge and they merely sketched them out, going through the motions. At any break, Fionna and Larry paired off, crouched on the side seats. Gary and Lynda also sat together, but Lynda had a more important part and was called back on stage frequently, so that Gary was then left isolated. The actors had their own seating area to which they returned when not performing. Territory was very clearly marked:

> It is the case that two or more individuals may together possess the same territory, jointly laying claim to it in the name of their collectivity. (Goffman, 1971, p. 57)[1]

It was obvious that disquieting undercurrents were affecting the rehearsal. Stuart laboured on. The actors maintained a camaraderie amongst themselves, even at one point converting their dance sequence into a Zorba routine.

[1] The concept of territoriality is, of course, drawn from ethology. It has been extended to include human behaviour, notably by Ardray, R., *The Territorial Imperative*, New York: Athenium, 1966. For an interesting short article on the significance of seating arrangements see R. Sommer 'Further Studies in Small Group Ecology'. In J. Laver & S. Hutcheson (Eds) *Communication in Face to Face Interaction* Harmondsworth: Penguin, 1972.

The dancers looked coldly on, dispirited and sullen. Larry came over and said, 'Well, I'm certainly glad to see *you*', with meaningful emphasis on the *you* which suggested he was at odds with everyone else. The stage manager came by and Gary said, 'Can we have this place swept?' The stage manager said it had been done. Gary said that he had got some glass in his toe. He crouched at Lynda's feet, inspecting his toe every so often. The contrast between the actors, struggling with unusual demands but meeting requirements with good humoured resilience, even exuberance in the Zorba sequence, and the depressed dancers came over with striking clarity. I was seeing not the enthusiastic and integrated group of people working on a joint venture which I had expected. Nor was I seeing two groups, actors and dancers, in profitable interaction. The actors were cohesive and positive, the dancers dispirited and fragmented.

Because the physical context of behaviour is important, I have described the Traverse auditorium. But there was a broader physical context which contributed to the situation I witnessed. November 1973 was the period of the threatened miners' strike. Electricity supplies had been cut and public buildings were gloomy and icy cold. Indeed, I had gone first to a church hall half a mile from the Traverse where I had expected to find the group rehearsing. Instead, they had been forced to abandon the hall as it was too cold to work in. The theatre was marginally warmer, but oddly combined a visually suffocating claustrophobia with a chill dankness.

Though I could perceive that the dancers were dispirited and though I realised that physical conditions were very trying, I could not begin to understand what I had seen until I had arranged for further tape recorded accounts. Witnessing manifest behaviour is not enough: it is necessary to share, through talk, the view-point of the person behaving. The evidence which follows is from individual accounts.

The arduous physical conditions had certainly contributed to the situation and more than I had realised:

LYNDA I didn't think the Traverse would be quite so small. I was expecting a stage with the audience in front. Instead they're all round and on top. This is certainly part of the problem. You know, all the frustration of having to cramp your movements and climb over legs and bump into people.

LARRY The cold is terrific. It really is. It's so hard to get moving at 10 o'clock in the morning when it's that cold, no matter how many pairs of tights you put on.

GARY It's so hard to keep in condition. Now today we had a good class—we ran around so much that we kept warm. But every time I stand up after I've been sitting I start limping. It's just that muscles get really cold and when you start leaping about you start tearing muscles.

The cold, which I had recognised as a source of discomfort, was to the dancers a very real professional hazard.

But their despondency arose from more complex issues. In Glasgow they had established an almost cosy cohesion, training day after day with Stuart and devising material for the future ten-week tour. They were dependent on him for the structuring of each day. *Columba* was, in anticipation, an exciting interlude. In reality it proved a powerful but disintegrating experience.

Because of the complexity of evolving a script which allowed for music and dance, constant revision was necessary up to the last moment. Mike Okrent, artistic director of the Traverse, had to be away for much of the period because of problems with a London production. Increasingly therefore, Stuart found himself involved not only with choreographing the dances but directing the actors. Because the aim was an integrated mixed media production, not only were the musicians and actors to 'dance', but, hopefully, the dancers were to act. As it worked out, Bob, the musician and Lynda were the only two to secure speaking roles. Gary, who had been auditioned by Mike Okrent for the important part of the Angel, was not accepted. With three weeks to go before the opening, Stuart took over this role. Instead, therefore, of concentrating on the choreography, as planned, he found himself carrying additional responsibility for a specific acting part and much of the overall direction. This dissonance between expectation and the actual sequence of events imposed severe strains.

Movable Workshop was no longer an entity, with fixed boundaries. Actors were dancing and Bob, Lynda and Stuart were acting. The clear differentiation of group membership through roles was gone. Those remaining within the original boundary had shrunk to three:

FIONNA Lynda's got a part. She's involved with both parties, but her being involved so much takes her away from the group. We're no longer four, we're three.

GARY I was working with Lynda a lot in Glasgow, but she has a part in the play, you see. So when she's not working I don't feel I can ask her to work because she's working so much. She's really tired. With Lynda, I feel sort of separated from her just because she has this role.

Lynda was herself strongly conscious that her acting part had cut her off from the others:

'For myself, I'm involved in the acting and in the dancing so I've got the best of both worlds so I'm happy in it. But I feel very unhappy because I feel as though I'm out of the group and they're out of the whole thing. It's terribly frustrating. I don't know which way to go. Because I'm happy—but I can see why the other three aren't happy. And I don't like the feeling, "I'm all right, Jack." Yet I feel sort of two faced if I say to the others, "I understand. I know how you feel." It seems a bit condescending or something.'

If Lynda's defection was disturbing, then the loss of Stuart was very much more so:

LARRY Stuart's now taken a role in the play which can't help but take some of his energies away from what we've got to do. I mean I admit that he's doing more work as an administrator than anyone I've seen. He's done more preparation even of the actors and they're happy and he's working very hard but I think he tends to forget that it's this group that he's meant to be launching. Because I think it's required in dancing that you do have a person you look up to and that—you know—if he's happy and things are going well then you feel that way as well. And it's not really worked out that way. In a way what we felt was that he was going to be our representative as it were, and it hasn't turned out that way at all.

FIONNA Stuart's got so many things on his mind. And obviously we're demanding his attention as well— feeling a bit neglected because we're feeling insecure at the moment because we've lost one of our group and the director of our group and suddenly there's just three of us and what are we going to do all afternoon. I know it's a matter of self-discipline but I think we're just surprised to find ourselves in that situation.

The person who had the most difficult task in coming to terms with the new situation was, of course, Gary, who had to deal not only with the general sense of insecurity but the particular disappointment of not being accepted for the speaking part of the Angel:

GARY I think actually the biggest problem we all feel now is with Stuart, which is really funny because when we were in Glasgow I felt very good about working with him. But Stuart isn't really concerned with us at the moment—he's got other things going on—there's his part plus working out the whole play . . . I guess there was also a little jealousy there because it originally was supposed to be a role that I would play. But because of my accent and also because Stuart is much more interesting on stage as an actor than I am they decided to use him. I wasn't really upset—I mean I wasn't really jealous of Stuart but I was upset not to have a part because suddenly I felt that I had no involvement in the play at all. I was a little bit relieved as well because I'd never done anything like that before but I was sort of . . . It's hard to see things very clearly.

'Well, you saw that clearly because you've been able to say, "Perhaps I was a bit jealous".'

GARY Just pre-packed psychology, perhaps. Also talking into the tape recorder I suddenly get very objective about everything—make more sense of it all.

The construction of social reality through talk with 'significant others' is an ongoing dynamic process.[2] Gary's comment shows that not only are the dancers through mutual conversation engaged in this activity. The talking into the tape machine is also part of the process, producing yet another version which Gary recognises as a construct—'I make more sense of it all.'

With boundaries broached and infiltration occurring from both sides the dancers experienced a strong identity crisis. The actors, who had incorporated three of their members, were professionally experienced and had a specific script to work from which ensured that each had a 'Character' to project. The dancers had no specific roles but were pagans, monks, druids as required. Because of the fragmentation of rehearsals inevitable in a mixed media production, and intensified by the initial use of two buildings, the dancers worked on small segments without gaining an over-view of the whole. Inevitably they questioned the value of their dances and voiced the suspicion that the play could stand on its own, that they could dispensed with without loss:

[2] The phrase is from Peter Berger and Hansfried Kellner's article, 'Marriage and the Construction of Reality'. In H. P. Dreitsel (Ed) *Recent Sociology* No. 2, London: Collier-Macmillan Ltd, 1970.

'The plausibility and stability of the world, as socially defined, is dependent upon the strength and continuity of significant relationships in which conversation about this world can be continually carried on. Or, to put it a little differently: the reality of the world is sustained through conversation with significant others.'

GARY I like the actors very much. They're good actors, you
see. I think the play would be fine without the dance
and music at all. It's a very well written play and could
be done quite well. I think the music is going to be
nice. I think the dancing will be all right as well, it's
just . . . Someone comes in and sees us and says 'Oh,
that dancing was nice.' But that's the problem, 'nice'.
I think it's maybe just an ego thing because being a
dancer you have to be on stage and recognised as a
dancer. When there are just two you are, but when
you are thumping around in the back somewhere
being a druid or a monk, I think that's what upsets
me the most. It's like experience in an opera.

In view of the tensions being generated, Larry used a highly
significant image in his attempt to explain the situation:

I find it very difficult dancing in something that's not
a dance. In other words it's a play and we are being
fitted in in certain sections. It's rather like being a
storm in the background.

Fionna struggled perceptively to analyse the nature of the
problem:

Last week the dancers were down at the Church Hall
and the actors were up at the theatre and we didn't see
the other half and that was very bad in a way. You
don't feel involved at all. The dances that we are doing
aren't demanding anything of us. It's very un-
satisfying in that respect, because with the actors
they've got the acting as well as the dance. There are
sections where the actors and dancers are together
and the dance has been simplified a great deal to basic
movements. Of course there is quite a lot for the
actors to manage—it's very demanding for them.
Today when we ran through the whole scene we just
felt like film extras—just coming on and dancing a

few fiddly bits and going off, because there's no satisfaction in what we're doing. I think mostly because we've no identity. We know we're druids in one part and part of a crowd in the next but we've no individual identity so there's no reason why we should want to dance. And you know, being dancers that makes an awful lot of difference. It's just today I felt it and I suddenly thought, 'Perhaps that's what's wrong.' We were talking today and saying 'Would it be more satisfying perhaps—although not possible—but if you had nothing to do in the whole thing except one part where you come on as someone?'

What is being searched for and desired is not, of course, merely an identity in the play. It is the lost identity of the group, experienced in Glasgow when boundaries were intact, but now fragmented, dissipated. Lynda, who says of herself 'I'm involved in the acting and in the dancing so I've got the best of both worlds', knows about this loss:

The feeling is—even I get the feeling—that we are not working together as a dance group any more. One feels a bit that one's being called up almost as an extra for this one play and then we'll all go home and disperse and it's nothing to do with being a group.

What was impressive was the way these relatively in-experienced young dancers struggled to express and understand their difficulties. Yet the struggle to understand problems is only a stage towards dealing with them and does not mean that you can cope with them adequately, as Gary was well aware in the following exchange:

'I can see your problems and talking them through possibly makes them sharper.'

GARY It makes them seem a little silly, a little petty.

'I said "sharper". I made no value judgement.'

GARY I know, but to myself when I talk about them they
seem a bit childish, but yet when I'm actually there
doing it it doesn't seem that way at all.

'It does not seem that way at all' because the feelings which
the dancers were experiencing could very accurately be
characterised as childish but were certainly not petty. Feelings
of outraged dependency, of jealousy of strong rivals who have
appropriated the leader and who dominate the situation so
that everything must be tailored to *their* needs—such feelings
are powerful rather than petty. Even 'pre-packed psychology'
is adequate to demonstrate that the *Columba* situation was
fraught with very real difficulties.

The one person who seemed able to concentrate on the task
in hand without stress was Bob. His peripheral position
enabled him to move easily across the boundaries so that he
managed triple responsibilities with evident enjoyment. As
one of the *Movable Workshop* group, he had loyalties to the
original company. As musician, he collaborated with the
composer, Peter Russel Brewis and the third of the trio, a
fiddler. He also had an acting role in the play. So for him
Columba offered rich opportunities which he was thoroughly
enjoying:

> I wanted a speaking part and I got one, so that was
> good because I like to participate fully. The music to
> the production is very good so professionally I like the
> show.

Bob's independence seemed acknowledged by all group
members. He was allowed to move from group to group in the
work situation without the stress of disrupted loyalties which
disturbed the others.

The following diagram will highlight the problem of inter
and intra-group relationships which the production posed.

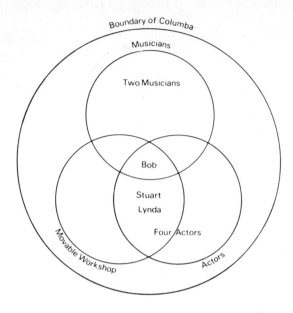

Given these problems, it was not surprising that Larry's 'storms' refused to stay in the background but broke over head. Mutual recriminations, attacks not only on Stuart and on the dance material but, by Gary and Larry, on the girls for failing to appear at a class, showed the extent of the sense of disintegration, a sense which culminated in Larry offering his resignation. Stuart, who had been well aware of the difficulties posed by the production, was nevertheless shocked by this evidence of collapse of morale:

> What was terribly disappointing was feeling that they thought I didn't know that it was difficult. It's incredibly difficult. The space is extremely limited. These black walls. Freezing cold for dancers to dance in. They turn up frozen to death. It takes forever to warm up and when you stop for a break you freeze again. Hideous conditions. But as I said today, 'We are not running a therapy group. We are running a professional company and we must behave as

professionals. If you find a thing difficult you must make the best of it. I find it difficult.' I felt very hostile towards them because I really felt there was a me and them situation growing up.

'How do you think it has grown up? What has contributed to it?'

STUART   I must assume fifty per cent of that responsibility. I think it isn't as they thought it would be. One of the problems is that because I'm playing the angel it means I have to be away much more. The work's exciting for me but for them it means they are without me for a lot of the time. So I think the situation is they miss me and I have betrayed Gary by playing the angel, betrayed them all. Larry hates anything like this kind of work. I think they all feel they are extras, that they come on and do their dance and go off. But in staggered rehearsals there's no other way. I said to them all today, 'Its going to get worse. It's not going to get better. It's going to get worse and we just have to slave away and stick together and work it.'

The open acknowledgement of difficulties led to an improved situation. At the next rehearsal, December 5th, the dancers were performing alone, without the actors. Stuart was directing from a raised chair, symbolically and actually in control. A pagan jig was being evolved to an exhilarating tune on the fiddle. The dance was both original and traditional, folksy yet unexpected—a refreshing solution to a difficult creative problem. The dancers were very committed to the work task, obviously physically tired but with no apathy or resistance. Indeed at one point they exaggerated a particular sequence of stiff, angular movements into a Dalek parody. The sense of fun underlying the actors' Zorba routine had revived in the dancers. The week before I had been given strong indications that I was needed—as a repository for confessions and gloomy outpourings. This week I was politely on the fringe—the group had other business. Indeed, there was a sheepish half-serious, half-humorous suggestion from Gary that I might wipe out last week's tapes. The only such suggestion, incidentally, in the whole of the enquiry. I was now the repository for things best unsaid—wiped out—and therefore a source of slight embarrassment.

It would be wrong to suggest that difficulties were resolved merely by being acknowledged. The group was subjected to powerful stresses which continued to operate throughout the entire production. I hope to show by my analysis of these events that these severe strains would have been felt by any work group, irrespective of the individual talents and personalities of the members. Moods continued to fluctuate violently. Larry, who had expressed much of the group's hostility to the particular production, injured himself and was unable to perform. The premature resignation thus became a reality through an accident which, like many, seemed to serve a non-accidental purpose. Larry's departure brought some relief, but again considerable recrimination and self doubt —had enough been done to retain him?

Columba opened on December 12th and ran for a highly successful three week season.

It is possible to explain the vicissitudes of *Movable Workshop* on the developmental model put forward by Tuckman (1970) in *Group Processes*. He surveys existing studies and classifies them according to three settings:

(1) Group Therapy Setting.
(2) Human Relations Training Group (T. Group) Setting.
(3) Natural Group Setting.   ⎫
    Laboratory Task Setting.   ⎭

The latter two are combined on the dubious ground of the small number of studies in each. He follows Bales and earlier workers in distinguishing between the task oriented functions of groups and the social-emotional-integrative functions.[3] He then offers the following model as a:

> ... conceptualisation of changes in group behaviour, in both social and task realms, across all group settings over time.

Stage
I   Testing and dependence (social realm)
        Orientation to the task (task realm)
Stage
II   Intra-group conflict (social realm)
        Emotional response to task demands (task realm)
Stage
III   Development of group cohesion (social realm)
        Open exchange of relevant interpretations and opinions (task realm)
Stage
IV   Functional role-relatedness (social realm)
        Emergence of solutions (task realm)

An overview of the existing literature reveals that:

> ... the suggested sequence appeared to hold up under widely varied conditions of group composition, duration of group life and specific group task' though it must be assumed that 'there is a finite range of conditions beyond which the sequence of development is altered.' (Tuckman, 1970, p. 347).

Tuckman neatly summarises the developmental sequence deduced from the literature as *Forming* (Stage I) *Storming* (Stage 2) *Norming* (Stage 3) and *Performing* (Stage IV).

The attractiveness of the model in relation to what has already been written about *Movable Workshop* will be

---

[3] See Bales, R. F., The equilibrium problem in small groups. In T. Parsons, R. F. Bales and E. A. Shils (Eds) *Working Papers in the Theory of Action*. New York: Free Press, 1953; Bales, R. F., *Interaction Process Analysis: A Method for the Study of Small Groups*. New York: Addison-Wesley, 1950; Deutch, M. A., A theory of co-operation and competition *Human Relations,* 1949, 2, 129-52; Jennings, H. H., Sociometric differentiation of the psyche group and sociogroup, *Sociometry,* 1947, 10, 71-9.

immediately apparent. The Glasgow period constitutes the 'Forming' stage when members look to a leader for guidance and support in the new situation, and attempt to determine the nature of the task and the way in which the group will be utilised to accomplish the task. *Columba* constitutes the 'Storming' stage when group members express hostility towards each other and to the leader, and react emotionally and with resistance to the demands of the task. We can then look forward to a period of 'norming' and 'performing' as the group embark on their ten week tour of the schools.

Seductive though the model is, there is a major flaw in its application. A developmental model has validity in relation to child development because the chronological time-sequence is fixed and behaviours can legitimately be segmented as characterising 2 – 5 year olds, 5 – 7 year olds etc. The life of a group in relation to a task can vary from two hours for a laboratory group to two years for a therapy group. How appropriate is a developmental model which seeks to deduce general characteristic stages within such absurdly divergent time spans? It is no answer to say that processes are compressed or extended according to the anticipated life span of the group. Had my research ended in November '73, I could have found evidence of 'forming' 'storming' 'norming' in the first two months of *Movable Workshop's* life. I suspect in all sustained groups the existence of cyclic processes in which members presented with a task will manifest orienting, conflict and problem-solving behaviours irrespective of the duration of the group's existence. According to the nature of the task, conflict may well recur in a group which in terms of its chronological life-span should have reached the 'problem solving' stage, leaving the emotional dependency stage behind.

So the neat application of a developmental model must be resisted since it assumes that the stages of progression will follow the researcher's time span, whether that be two hours or two years. Instead I would suggest a cyclic model with group reactions varying according to the demands of the task. Having acknowledged this, however, I then recognise with

Tuckman that common sense suggests that at various stages in the group's life certain ways of reacting are likely to predominate. Thus 'forming' is obviously an initial activity and can only recur if and when the group acquires new members and/or new tasks. Because of the insecurity engendered by strange situations and demands, members will manifest the maximum dependency at this stage. Once the initial strangeness is overcome, then any group is likely to manifest 'storming' behaviours in the sense that individuals will assert themselves, discover they dislike aspects of each other and the task, and will express this. Knowledge that the group will disintegrate and the task be unfulfilled generally leads to modifications of behaviour which allow the group to survive and the task to be accomplished. As these latter situations occur and recur in cyclic sequence, the group may well reach a stage of sufficient self knowledge to be able to reduce storming and increase its problem solving powers. *Movable Workshop* was no exception to the common-sense pattern I have indicated. In Glasgow its members showed considerable initial dependency on Stuart Hopps:

> I've learned how they depended on me a great deal more than I realised. I've learned how I depend on them more than I realised, but in a different way.

This dependence was maintained over a period of several weeks because the job requirements could only be known and interpreted by Stuart. After the move to Edinburgh, the particular nature of the *Columba* task ensured that the emergence from a dependency situation would be especially painful. To summarise:

(1) The group had not yet established its public identity. It's self image was dependent on an audience recognising it as *Movable Workshop* and applauding what it recognised. For two months the members worked in daily contact on a programme designed to ensure this recognition. Who the audience were likely to be and what they were likely to require could only be mediated by Stuart Hopps.

(2) In late November members had to switch from this task to the task of implementing a script for a mixed media production.

(3) This involved working with a more mature and experienced group of actors.

(4) Three members of the group achieved acting roles, which weakened their membership of *Movable Workshop*.

(5) One of these was Stuart Hopps. The demands of choreography, acting and directing were so strenuous that he had little time to devote exclusively to the dancers. They felt they had lost their mediator, their 'representative'.

(6) Within the production, the three remaining dancers were called upon to assume a variety of roles—pagans, monks, druids. The original group identity was lost and no new identity could be found in the play.

(7) The applause of the audience would not be a recognition of *Movable Workshop,* but of the cast of *Columba.*

So the demands of the saint imposed a severe identity crisis. In this situation of stress the group manifested behaviours which can certainly be designated as 'storming' but which are perhaps, more deeply understood by reference to Bion's theories. These were evolved during the late 1940s and early 1950s and were based on his pioneer work as psychiatrist with small groups in the therapeutic setting of the Tavistock clinic, or with training groups of industrialists, administrators and educationalists at the Tavistock Institute of Human Relations. These theories have been legitimately criticised by, for instance, Michael Sherwood, (1964) in a stringent article in *Human Relations.* Nevertheless, their explanatory power is considerable. I shall utilise Richardon's (1967, p. 54) succinct account of them:

> At times his groups were dominated by their need for one person on whom to depend, and they would try to set up this person as omniscient and infallible. At other times they appeared to be relying on a pair, as if in the hope that this pair might produce the new magical leader of the future. And at other times they were concerned only to preserve their own identity by fighting something or running away from it.

Manifestations of these 'unconscious needs', or, in Bion's terms, 'basic assumptions' of 'dependency', 'pairing' and 'fight-flight' will be readily apparent in the evidence I have mustered. It was perhaps only appropriate that Larry should carry his 'fight-flight' leadership to its logical conclusion!

Certain general principles emerge from this consideration of *Movable Workshop's* problems:

(1) Firstly, a newly formed group is vulnerable, particularly so if recruitment has presented problems. It needs to succeed at some task in order to establish its identity both to its own members and to people outside its boundary.

(2) If it is compelled by circumstances to interact with a more powerful and experienced group before it has accomplished (1), then the stress will induce strong feelings of disintegration.

(3) Ideally, such interactions should be deferred until the group has achieved recognition in its own right.

Of course, the pressure of events prevents our operating an ideal situation. Stuart Hopps was well aware that ideally *Columba* should have followed the ten week tour of schools, not preceded it. But booking schedules are inflexible: *Columba* was planned for the Christmas season at the Traverse as early as May, '73. The only choice open was to produce *Columba* without *Movable Workshop,* and create the new company in January '74. Or create the company in October '73 and expose it to the demands of a complex mixed-media production somewhat prematurely. The second choice offered more prestige to the newly formed group, and a unique learning opportunity:

STUART It was important for us—for *Movable Workshop*—to do it. As I said earlier, the timing is unfortunate and it would have been nice if it had come later in the year. If it had come after the ten week tour we would be sick and tired of doing the dances we are doing and ready for something new—ready for Edinburgh, ready to live in a new environment and ready for new faces. But it couldn't. It had to come now. So I think it was still right to do it and I think we've learned a lot from it.

In the pressure of real life situations, work groups may frequently be compelled to undertake tasks which differ somewhat from those for which they have been training, and which expose them to infiltration from others before their own group identities have been established. In such situations stresses will occur irrespective of the personnel forming such groups. Conflict and flight from the task will ensue, and this is no reflection on the competencies and capacities of group members. Nor, if flight is checked, does continuing conflict necessarily mean that the task will be badly accomplished. There is ample evidence of groups with inner strains nevertheless achieving high levels of effectiveness.[4] An understanding of the forces at work can help, however, to a tolerance of the inevitable difficulties, to the prevention of destructive impulses, and to the conscious utilisation of the 'basic assumptions'. It is because of this that material from the tapes, far from being wiped out, is offered here as a source of insight.

[4] See, for instance, Lenk, Hans, Top performance despite internal conflicts. In J. W. Loy & G. S. Kenyon (Eds) *Sport, Culture & Society*. New York: Macmillan, 1969. Also Coser, Lewis, A., *The Functions of Social Conflict*, New York: Routledge & Kegan Paul, 1965. For an interesting discussion of 'groups-in-controlled-tension' see Elias, N. & Dunning E., Dynamics of Sport Groups with special reference to Football. In E. Dunning (Ed), *The Sociology of Sport*. London: Frank Cass & Co Ltd, 1971.

4

COLUMBA AND REALITY

Differing Viewpoints

Columba opened on December 20th and for three weeks the script, the music, the dances were enacted nightly by the cast of twelve. As a symbol of the integrative nature of the production the programme contained no details of who did what: actors, dancers and musicians were merely listed in alphabetical order as 'The Company'. This deliberately cultivated role-versatility which led to virtual anonymity symbolised the intention of the playwright and the producers to offer *not* a spoken script with some additional dance and music, but an artistic fusion of all three. The programme is a tangible piece of documentary evidence as to intention: a message to performers and audience as to how they are to view the play.

What constituted the reality of the experience of *Columba* for the various people who participated, either as players or audience? A tangible script, written music, choreographed dances exist as 'facts' in the symbolic world of art. 'Art is the creation of forms, symbolic of human feeling' (Langer, 1953, p. 40). The activation of these in a production forces us to shift into the subjective world of interaction and relationships:

> The social world is a subject and not an object world. It does not constitute a reality sui generis divorced from the human beings who constitute its membership. Rather, the social world is the existential product of human activity and is sustained and changed by such activity. (Walsh, 1972, p. 18.)

One surprising feature of this social world was that to the actors, as reported by the dancers, it seemed a very cohesive one. The internal dissentions of *Movable Workshop* were absorbed in the integration of the larger group. What initially were rival and potentially disruptive interests merged into a common purpose under the pressures and excitements of actual performance. Thus Fionna reported that she and Lynda had shared a dressing room with Deborah Benzimra, who played Brigid, an Irish girl. Deborah had asserted that she had never met a company which had jelled so successfully for a play. Usually it was a case of people reading their own parts, then just coming together on stage, but she felt that this group was different. Really friendly contacts had been made. This account of the actors' viewpoint was reinforced by evidence from Peter Allen. Peter had been summoned to join the *Movable Workshop* a week before the end of the run of *Columba,* and naturally spent much of that week at the Traverse:

> Actors don't form groups that much. They come together, they work for the period of the production and they're out again on their various ways, and this doesn't encourage them to form close knit groups. I think it might be a bad thing for them in some respects if they did, because you're always leaving and making new relationships again and going on. I've always found professional actors—the few I have met—very cold. But here I got that friendly atmosphere. I was expecting the actors to be a bit cold to me because I'd not been involved at all, but they all

said, 'Oh, hello, you're the new member of the group, are you?' and things like that.

Supplementary 'factual' evidence showed that relationships were maintained beyond the run of the play, the musicians arranging to come to see *Movable Workshop's* performance and Christopher Burgess, who took the part of Columba, accepting an invitation to give a talk at the college where a friend of Fionna's was following a course on film technology. I had seen a marked potential for conflict inherent in the intra-group relationships but this had been restrained by other factors. One of these was the existence of a 'superordinate goal'. Sherif (1966, p. 93) has demonstrated how a superordinate goal, that is, a goal with an appeal for members of each group 'but that neither group can achieve without participation of the other' can successfully bring about co-operation and cohesion. Such a goal was the performance of *Columba*. Another factor was that the actors danced and musicians danced and acted, so that empathy developed between the various sub-groups. *Movable Workshop's* sense of identity was painfully weakened, but a compensation was that the polarisation of actors versus dancers versus musicians, which could have occurred had internal boundaries been maintained, was avoided. The dancers of *Movable Workshop* reported that, in spite of their problems, for the rest of the company *Columba* was a warm and cohesive experience. The supplementary evidence confirms their accounts.

But how was it experienced by the dancers themselves? As a period of continuing stress, when constant reappraisals of individuals and relationships had to be coped with:

LYNDA I saw new people and that surprised me.

'And did those new people still seem new today?'

LYNDA Yes, I think so, but less new. I'm getting used to them again.

As for the play itself, this was perceived through the prism of fluctuating moods, and in the light of the opportunities or frustrations it offered to individual aspirations:

LYNDA For me, the enjoyable outweighs the painful. I don't see myself either as a brilliant dancer or a brilliant actress but I think I can tackle both. If I were more involved in wanting to be a superb dancer then I think I would find *Columba* much more difficult because I would just want to dance. But I like the Traverse and working with actors, perhaps because I've done drama before. All through my life my father used to conduct theatre orchestras so I've always been in theatre things—grease paint and all that. I was in amateur dramatics at school. I went to Dartington in fact to do drama, not to do dance at all and I changed when I was there. So I'm quite excited by *Columba*. I'm more happy than unhappy. But that's leaving aside the painfulness of others being unhappy.

FIONNA We feel we are just being the chorus group behind. The dances are all so short. You get going on a reel—it's beautiful music and super to dance to and you just get started and you're off again. I think I am probably finding it less frustrating than Gary who's had more experience of this sort of thing. Because it's a new experience I find it exciting for that reason. I feel that for me the positives outweigh the negatives. But as a satisfactory experience in terms of dance, I'm not so sure.

GARY The dancing parts are so small and they're extras in the play. And as a dancer it's almost like being in the chorus line at Las Vegas—we come on, we bring actors on and run off—then suddenly we tear round the stage and slip off again—it's almost like the parades in Shakespeare to get dead bodies on and off. We're sort of just filling up the stage. When the saint first comes to the island there are pagans there, so do a little pagan dance. Come back on as monks. Then we're peasants. Whenever there's a crowd wanted on stage bring on the dancers. And that's what we do. I think that's what upsets me.

STUART It's very hard to devise a cultural world. You can read about it but the kinetic source of energy is lost. We don't even know what the Greek dances were. So *Columba*—well! A nightmare. Very exciting. A miracle.

When I saw the production myself, in the New Year, I carried to the performance all the impressions and preconceptions derived from fragmented observation and from the diverse comments of the dancers. Because I had watched the movement sections in rehearsals and heard nothing of the script, I feared that the topic of a saint's life would produce a derivative text, flaccid with the empty solemnity of 'religious' drama. Instead the remote conflicts between paganism and a Celtic Christianity which could still encompass human sacrifice were given immediacy by the vivacity of the language. Earthy, god-driven, humorous yet passionately serious, Columba, accompanied by his ambiguous Angel, was a character of unexpected verve and relevance. His pilgrimage to his death in old age was consistently intriguing and ultimately moving. The tiny Traverse auditorium, formerly so claustrophobic, was invested with a spacious calm by Geoffrey Scott's austere set, a rock on which Columba's cross was raised. The music, dance and visual effects seemed powerfully to reinforce and supplement the spoken script. Although there was some unevenness, moments when intention seemed not to be fully realised, these, contrary to my expectations, arose from the script, not from dichotomies between dance and text. Of the chorus line analogies, of the quick spurts on and off stage so strongly felt by the performers I was quite unaware, merged as the dance episodes were in the total impact of a particular scene. My view of *Columba* from the third level of the Traverse auditorium was of a production not at every point surely and sufficiently realised, but consistently interesting and exploiting, with an exhilerating success in view of my anticipatory fears, the resources of speech, music and the dance.

So where was the real *Columba*? Mine, with its weight of patchy foreknowledge, was different from that of the other members of the audience who came perhaps with a burden of pre-conceptions about Iona, but fresh to the theatrical experience. Spectators' *Columba* was different from Performers' *Columba* and Actors' *Columba* differed from Dancers', and Lynda's differed from Gary's. So will the real Columba step forward?

Perhaps this is the real *Columba* emerging from the critics' responses. After all, reviews constitute documentary evidence!

It is a splendid idea to mingle a theatre company and a ballet one for a show. I hope the Traverse and Scottish Theatre Ballet's *Movable Workshop* follow up *Columba* with another production sometime. The work uses the techniques of both to show the saint from his coming to Iona to the end of his life. Music, noise, rhythm, speech, movement, dance are all put to the telling and the showing. After *Beowulf* last year I was excited by the way all these were used and anticipated *Columba* with great pleasure. Unfortunately, the unity, the tension, the *building* of *Beowulf* are not to be found here. It is very episodic and rather flat, raised by the dancing and allowed to fall again . . . Whirling robes, weirdly hairy druids leaping about the stage, lighting effects, beautiful body-shapes, candles, all these were good to experience. In a rather thin play theatrical magic helps. (*Arts Theatre.*)

S. Columba was bearing a sword and a spade when he strode onto the stage of the Traverse Theatre in Ediburgh last night. This raised expectations that he was going to be portrayed as a warrior and a workman—pacifier of the pagan Picts and builder of churches, and more a man of action than of contemplation. But the character who emerged from C. P. Taylor's 'Columba' was neither one thing nor the other.

As played by Christopher Burgess, he resembled a commercial traveller rather than a missionary . . . The dancers went through some fairly conventional motions, punctuating and occasionally enlivening the four scenes from S. Columba's life. (Allen Wright. *The Scotsman.*)

Perhaps my hopes were too high: at any rate this retelling of the planting of the first Christian Cross on Scottish soil is stimulating, endearing, amusing and exasperating in about equal measure . . .

What is very good is the sense of immediacy. This Saint Columba is not a plaster figure, but of the earth . . . Now humorously tolerant, now irascible with the people he calls his family, Columba is torn between loving humanity as an idea and finding himself all too often alienated by the reality.

The music by Peter Russell Brewis is an apt blend of strange unearthly sounds and rollicking dancing tunes (the Druid's battle and ritual are all stylised in dance.) (Cordelia Oliver. *The Guardian*)

The picture of Columba is an essentially humanistic one—not an ideal, let alone a plaster saint. As people keep saying to him 'For a Saint, you're an awful coarse man.' So Columba is the Irish peasant, whose communion with God is a fumbling thing and whose faith in the Father and his family of monks is often sorely tried. He's near enough to pagan times to want a disciple entombed alive in the church foundations to make the building stand—but modest enough to abrogate responsibilities for his miracles. It's a kind of lovable, glad, hippyness.

And it doesn't really add up to the essence that could justify the dedication and the scholarship and the genius that we know emanated from Iona. To me, Taylor's contribution is a kind of fun, but in the end inconsequential. For me, the justification for the show lies in the other arts—the acting, the dancing, the music and the stage picture. All four are fine. (Halla Beloff. *Radio Scotland*)

C. P. Taylor's new play, *Columba,* at the Traverse Theatre, Edinburgh, is an experience that is entirely robust and reviving. It is about the making of a community in Iona under the guidance of the Saint. It is a play of spiritual distinction—not that Mr Taylor sets out to achieve any such objective. He busies himself with the creation of a practical, sometimes irascible, stubborn man, who is frequently in doubt as to whether he is on the right lines, as are the ordinary men and women who come to him with their problems. These, which are taken from Columba's life story, are the substance of the play and the sense of all nature being alive to the old man is winningly conveyed by Christopher Burgess.

All the characters are warm with natural life: the final effect is not comic, but one of dignity, achieved by a combination of forces, by dances and music of *Movable Workshop* and by lighting and design. The production is a company achievement; the play gives a new stature to C. P. Taylor. (George Bruce, *Sunday Times.*)

It would seem that Critics' *Columba* is as diverse as the actors' or the dancers'. The critics are also perceiving through the prism of moods and in the light of expectations, anticipations, preconceptions and prejudices. Columba the character is seen as a commercial traveller, as a hippy peasant, as saint; the dances as theatrical magic which raise a flat play; as fairly conventional motions, punctuating and occasionally enlivening; as stylised narrative and ritual: the play as episodic and flat, as stimulating and exasperating, as a kind of fun but inconsequential, as a play of spiritual distinction. It is not only that opinions vary as to the *value* of what they have perceived. They would seem to have perceived different things.

Horner and Bühler (1969, pp. 55-73) in an article on existential and humanist psychology, quote a statement of Kierkegaard's:

When we are dealing with human beings, no truth has reality by itself: it is always dependent upon the reality of the immediate relationship.

Their comment follows:

This is not to say that the existential view is that of the philosophical idealist, for facts are acknowledged as being real. A tree is a tree—although its meaning to the man who views it ('the truth') depends upon his relationship to it. Does it give him fruit or shade, or is it an obstacle in his path?

Similarly, though less metaphorically, Cicourel (1964, p. 220) asserts that:

> ... the actor's awareness and experience of an object are determined not only by the physical object as it is . . . given, but also by the imputations he assigns to it.

There is no need to spell out the implications of this in terms of a critic's, an actor's, a dancer's *Columba*. Nor in terms of Stuart's or Bob's or Gary's *Columba*. Or mine.

5

WHO REALLY BELONGS?

Integration and Cohesion

The period of initial recruitment, rehearsals and the presentation of *Columba* were a prelude to the major task for which the group had been formed, the ten week tour of schools, colleges and universities which extended from January 31st to April 10th '74. The theme of membership has already been treated, but it is logical to revive it at this juncture, not only because newcomers joined the company but because original memberships were affected by the transition to new tasks. The departure of Larry had made the acquisition of a second male dancer essential and, as already mentioned, Peter Allen who had auditioned in November was summoned in the New Year. I asserted in Chapter 2 that the method of recruitment affects the newcomer's relationship with the organisation he joins. Thus Peter, who experienced a delay between audition and membership, had to live with the question as to whether he would have been brought in had Larry not withdrawn:

> When I got here I couldn't help wondering if I'd only

been called up here to fill the gap. If Larry had stayed, I think perhaps I'd never have been called. It makes you very uneasy.

Since Larry *had* withdrawn, the query was unanswerable, and Peter, in spite of reassurances, had to live with the unease.

The other recruit was a third woman, Marita West. She was classically trained and had a range of professional experience. Stuart felt that she would provide some necessary strengths for the tour and presented her to the company as a *fait accompli,* without the rituals of auditions and discussion which had been utilised with Larry and Peter. The result was considerable initial wariness: the group had survived *Columba* and was reluctant to accommodate a newcomer. Marita overcame these reservations by a combination of professional aplomb and attractiveness of temperament:

FIONNA Peter fitted in very well. But we all had reservations about Marita. It's all right to say it now, but we did have reservations because she was just presented to us. 'Here's your new member.' Yet she's fitted in so well. I think having the strength—you know. It was a job to her as much as anything and she was going to do it.

GARY I wasn't sure about Marita coming at all. I thought she wasn't necessary. In a way it was just because I felt so good with the people we had got already. She was like a strange new person, and for the first week I'm sure we were all a bit cold to her.

LYNDA I think she has been incredible to have stood up because . . . We were nice to her as a person but we were a little closed group and we didn't see the point of having somebody else come in, basically. To have stood up to the first week before we got to know each other—well, she must have had a will of iron.

GARY Yeah. She sort of forced you to accept her.

LYNDA Had it been me arriving in that situation I'd have given up after the first day, I think.

GARY I think it was that we had just finished *Columba* and we felt very close knit and Lynda, Fionna and I had come through all that and it seemed such an imposition to have to deal with somebody else—it really did. But now I think she does add a very nice quality to the group. She's also a very different sort of person.

'In what way?'

LYNDA She's been teaching and dancing and looking after herself if you like. We've been training, and after that we've come straight into this in a group under surveillance. She's been out and about so she's a bit more confident in herself as herself.

GARY I think she's a very sweet person—very sort of soft. She's got the traditional feminine qualities. Modern dancers tend to be, not more earthy, but more down to earth in a way. I have a hard time seeing Marita whirling round on the floor.

LYNDA It's a more sexual thing, modern dance.

GARY Yeah—or unisexual.

LYNDA But she's so feminine.

GARY And all her dancing is very soft.

These extracts illustrate vividly the extreme cohesiveness which can develop between individuals who have survived a demanding task. A newcomer who has inevitably missed out on this baptism of fire is going to have difficulty gaining admission. The problem in Marita's case was intensified by her different background of classical training—something to be regarded with suspicion in view of the group's past history. Marita's combination of steely professional will with a delightful equanimity of temperament ensured her ultimate acceptance. When I asked if she had been aware of any problems, she replied without rancour:

But of course they wouldn't want me at first. They'd been working together very intensively. But I am quite used to adjusting to new situations and working with new people. It was just a case of getting on with the job.

The familiar nucleus of dancers with whom I had worked for three months was thus enlarged. Moreover, because of the requirements of touring, support staff in the form of a stage manager and a wardrobe mistress were appointed. Gavin Drummond answered an advertisement, was interviewed by the Assistant Administrator at Scottish Ballet, Geoffrey Macnab, and was offered the former post. Elizabeth Hammill (Lisa) after a term at a college of education, felt she had made a wrong choice of career and decided to follow a long held ambition to work in the theatre. She wrote on her own initiative to Scottish Ballet, was interviewed by the wardrobe mistress of the main company, and was offered the post with *Movable Workshop*. Job specialisation inevitably meant that initially these two felt apart from the dancers. Their work was essential to the group's functioning. Indeed, their presence reinforced the group sense of identity:

PETER When we left Glasgow we were in the 'bus together and all of a sudden that was it. We were on tour; I felt that we came together then.

FIONNA Yes, And it was also because we had our own wardrobe mistress and stage manager. We were a complete unit then.

Though essential, and recognised as belonging, yet neither Gavin nor Lisa shared in the intensity of performing out front. Their separation was reinforced by the physical fact that while the dancers travelled by minibus, they travelled separately driven by Gavin in the van containing the equipment and costumes. As Gavin said on the second day of the tour:

I get on very well with Lisa. Simply because we're both out of it. We've started being detached physically, too. We travel in the van together. We both didn't go to the party last night. (After the opening performance.) I think that was an extension of our own mental feeling that we are out of it. We're actually becoming dismembered.

Lisa's own strong sense of autonomy arose not only from independence of character but from the nature of her work task:

> Really, in one sense you're your own master as far as the wardrobe goes. You go out and buy what you think is right on an order sheet. To a certain extent they think, 'You're the wardrobe mistress and you know what you are doing.' You've five dancers but you've only one wardrobe mistress. They all depend on you to a certain extent. They say, 'What do you think Lisa?', and you've just got to take decisions. Actually I'm a very independent person so it suits me fine.

Thus role differentiation within the group led to subgroupings, with Lisa and Gavin asserting their individual contribution, or pairing on the basis of their 'non-dancing' tasks. Had *Movable Workshop* belied its title and remained in one location the possible 'dismemberment' which Gavin had sensed in the early stages might well have occurred. In large scale institutions and organisations. administrative, technical and support staff can become alienated from the front 'professionals' who directly implement official goals:

> The most basic principle of administrative authority and the most basic principle of authority based on knowledge—or professional authority—not only are not identical but are quite incompatible. (Etzione, 1964, p. 76).

In small groups a split between professional *v* administrative technical is very much less likely to happen, but it can still occur. Other elements in the touring situation, however, ensured that all *Movable Workshop's* limbs remained intact and fully articulated. Thus Gavin and Lisa travelled in a separate van, but this territory did not remain inviolate. Fionna, forced to stay behind in one town by illness, travelled in the van to rejoin the main group:

> I drove with them when I was off for two days. I took a four hour journey with them back from Galashiels. It was very strange. It was very nice but it was like a whole little world you didn't know was going on. You knew it was related to what we were doing but you saw everything from a different side.

This testifies to the separation of a group within a group, but reveals the friendly two-way interest which allowed empathy to develop. Bob, with the within group mobility which had always characterised him, decided partway through the tour to move from travelling with the dancers in the minibus to travelling in the van. His musical equipment was there, so in one sense this was a rational choice. Territorial changes carry, however, much more meaning than this. How far Bob was escaping from the pressures of the minibus with its seven occupants, how far succumbing to the attraction of Lisa's presence, only Bob would know, and he was ribbed on both counts. His shift, carried out imperturbably, provided yet another link between subgroups.

Finally, although there were two vehicles, places for working, eating and sleeping were identical. Apart from specific travelling time, all members were in virtual twenty four hour proximity. Not only did Gavin and Lisa share in the pressures of the work tasks, but they ate school lunches with the group, had dinner in the same hotels, had the same sleeping accommodation, got up to the same hotel breakfasts. With such intimate interaction at the social level, the sense of separation induced by job specialisation was diminished. Not only at the task level but at the sentient level,[1] Lisa and Gavin belonged:

[1] The distinction between the group as a social entity and the group as a task entity

GARY Gavin belongs because he joins in—he says things
—like in the discussion the other night.

FIONNA But Lisa understands us. She's very quick.

My conception of 'the group' had not only to be modified to
encompass the newcomers: it had to accommodate a further
readjustment. Geoffrey Macnab, as Assistant Administrator
of Theatre Ballet, had planned the programme of engagements for *Movable Workshop*. It was he who attended
to the legal aspects of membership, the contracts and salaries.
I had met him in order to discuss the administrative
background of the company. Yet in spite of all this knowledge
of his intimate connection with the group I had never thought
of him as a member of it, but as a peripheral figure operating
across the boundary with the main company. For this reason
he puts in no appearance in the earlier diagrams which show
the group as it was experienced at that stage. That my concept
of group membership corresponded with the dancers' is
apparent from the fact that Geoffrey never featured in the
early discussion material. I find this striking evidence of the
fact that a person whose services are administratively
essential can nevertheless fail to be acknowledged as a
member. Because he is not in day to day interaction, because
his task differs from the task of the face to face work group,
he may exist on the periphery, known more to the people
outside the boundary than to those within. With the start of
the tour, however, all this changed. Geoffrey interpreted his
task as administrator as not only to plan and to communicate
with outside bodies, but actually to accompany the group. It
was he who contacted staff in colleges and schools,
interviewed hotel receptionists, arranged the day to day
interactions with other organisations. As with Gavin and

has already been referred to in Chapter 3 in relation to Tuckman's developmental
model. This distinction is utilised by Miller, E. J. & Rice, A. K., *Systems of
Organisation: The Control of Task and Sentient Boundaries.* London: Tavistock,
1967, p. 18. They make a distinction between the 'task system', the formal structure
by means of which an organisation achieves its primary task, and the 'sentient system'
which directly commands the loyalty of members.

Lisa, he shared in the twenty four hour proximity of the travelling company. He not only rode in the mini-bus—he drove it. All this had considerable effects on existing relationships, particularly on patterns of leadership and I shall return to this in a later chapter where leadership is explored. It is sufficient to say at this stage that the group discovered it had a further member, one who had been involved since its inception but whose membership was only acknowledged after he moved into a situation of daily face to face interaction.

Thus the complete *Movable Workshop* group recruited for the ten week tour must be represented by a new diagram.

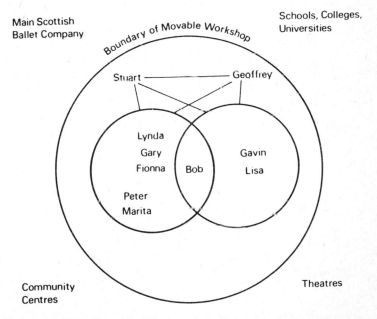

Group membership can be represented diagramatically, and this reification reveals those who belong at the task-oriented level in terms of legal contracts, salaries, responsibility for certain aspects of the job. The diagram can also imply certain sentient subgroupings in such things as the positioning of the dancers, the placing of Bob, and the relationship of Gavin, Lisa, Geoffrey etc. But there is an *experience* of membership which cannot be reified into diagramatic terms. It is possible to be technically a member of a group and yet remain very powerfully conscious of individuality and separateness:

> The relationship of the individual to his group varies: he may be a fully conforming member, or he may be unabsorbed, being physically in the group but not *of* it, an isolated unit who always has great difficulty in 'belonging' within any group (Brown, 1954, p. 175).

Indeed, the level and kind of balance struck between awareness of ego-centred needs and awareness of merged individuality into something that can be termed group identity will not only vary between individuals and between groups, but will vary within the same group. The feeling of 'belonging' in the full experiential sense will in some task groups never be achieved by any of those who are technically its members: in others it will fluctuate, being strongly apprehended in some situations and less powerfully felt at others. Laing (1967, pp. 71-2) has grappled with the problem of expressing this concept of the group as 'experienced' by its members:

> The being of any group from the point of view of the group members themselves is very curious. If I think of you and him as together with me, and others again as not with me, I have already formed two rudimentary syntheses, namely, *We* and *Them*. However, this private act of synthesis is not in itself a group. In order that *We* come into being as a group, it is necessary not only that I regard, let us say, you and him and me as *We*, but that you and he also think of us as *We*. I shall call such an act of experiencing a number of persons as a single collectivity an act of rudimentary group synthesis. In this case *We*, that is each of us, me you and him, have performed acts of rudimentary group synthesis. But at present these are simply three private acts of group synthesis. In order that a group really jell, I must realise that you think of yourself as one of Us, as I do, and that he thinks of himself as one of Us, as you and I do. I must ensure, furthermore that both you and he realise that I

think of myself with you and him, and you and he must ensure
likewise that the other two realise that this *We* is ubiquitous
among us, not simply a private illusion on my, your or his part,
shared between two of us but not all three . . .

The group, considered first of all from the point of view of the
experience of its own members, is not a social object out there in
space. It is the quite extraordinary being formed by each
person's synthesis of the same multiplicity into *We,* and each
person's synthesis of the multiplicity of syntheses.

This synthesis of multiplicity into 'We' will occur more
powerfully in some situations than others. I suggest that it is
particularly likely to occur when the very nature of the group
task demands not merely an aggregation of individual
contributions but their interplay and co-ordination. Thus a
dance group, where individuals are dependent on the
sensitivity, support and interaction of others, will experience
the 'We' more powerfully than a work-group which is meeting
production requirements by the summation of individual
outputs. This would also hold true of a 'team' in the games
situation whereas a 'team' of athletes could well remain a
conglomeration of individuals. Moreover, a dance group and
a games team enact this 'We-ness' in a ritualised public
performance, with 'Them' clearly present in terms of
spectators and, for the games team, opponents. Athletes, who
will be equally conscious of the 'Them', are usually involved in
an individual display. The particular dance-group, *Movable
Workshop,* were likely, however, to experience 'We-ness'
more strongly than a group performing set choreographies
since their programme involved improvisation and therefore
required a sensitivity and interaction beyond the activation of
fixed patterns. In this they were akin to a games team which,
in the rule-bound situation, is continually improvising. And
within *Movable Workshop* itself the level of intensity of 'We-
ness' would be likely to rise, as with a games team, in certain
key performances.

Striking confirmation of this assumption is provided by
reference to the opening performance of the entire tour. This
was held at Dunfermline College of Physical Education on

January 31st. During the day, members of the company conducted workshops with students in which dance ideas were explored through both movement and discussion. In the evening the first public performance took place before an audience of students, staff and outside visitors. The performance was designed to complement the workshops in that it, too, was intended as a learning experience. Thus items had been devised which demonstrated the way in which dances could be created from different stimuli—from poems, from shapes and from rhythms. The audience were not relegated solely to the role of spectators—at one point they were called upon to supply the rhythmic sounds to which the dancers improvised.

A spoken commentary by Stuart Hopps made explicit the various issues. Though several full scale dances were performed, including abstract and full costumed pieces, many items were designed to provide specific insights into training, choreography, the dance experience. Thus audience response was particularly important in that some sections would not 'work' without positive co-operation. So anticipatory tension was high. In the event, the audience proved warmly appreciative. Since most were students training to be physical education specialists it was an informed response and therefore all the more gratifying. I had watched this performance and had been aware that the dancers were responding with increasing confidence and zest as they sensed the approval. Their rapport both amongst themselves and with the audience was very apparent. Yet I missed entirely the significance of a tiny episode which to them was invested with a profound importance. This only emerged in discussion the next day. It is, of course, again of considerable methodological significance, a confirmation of the appropriateness of the theoretical stance adopted, that my observation of behaviour did not yield this evidence and that only through discussion did it emerge.

Fionna and Peter were talking to me of their reactions to the performance:

FIONNA I felt very pleased.

'Could you sense an audience reaction?'

FIONNA Oh yes—a very generous audience.
PETER Yes.

'How do you feel now, going out to do this together?'

PETER I feel good—confident.
FIONNA Yes, that was the nice thing about last night, feeling the group. Like in *Dance by Addition*—well, you know, we all say our names and then do our pieces. We usually just call out the names and in rehearsal we just say 'Gary', 'Lynda', 'Fionna'. But all five of us last night instead of just saying 'Fionna', we all said *'Fi-onna'* and we all did it.
PETER Yes, we all did. There was no cue. Everybody said it together. There was a feeling.
FIONNA There was no need for all of us to have said it like that, but we did. We were saying this today.
PETER And I could see Stuart out of the corner of my eye—he was delighted I think, by that. . . .
FIONNA I like the group now. I feel its a group rather than two or three or one. Especially last night.
PETER It was nice. There were so many little things we developed which we hadn't rehearsed. Some things can't develop until you have an audience and then you react to each other for the audience.

In objective terms what precisely had happened? One dancer's name had been called out with a particular humorous exaggerated intonation. To the dancers, this was a sign of their rapport. It had been done without cue. Because at the outset of the tour it was very necessary to feel a strong sense of solidarity this tiny event was seized on. It became a symbol of cohesiveness. It was talked about. 'We were saying this today.' Stuart was drawn into the rapport. 'I could see

Stuart out of the corner of my eye. He was delighted, I think, by that.'

A group about to embark on a challenging task needs to feel cohesive. This was particularly important for members of *Movable Workshop* in that the strains of *Columba* had proved disruptive. All members had made conscious efforts to repair relationships:

LYNDA We've been working and Stuart's been working to get back together again.

'How do you know about Stuart?'

LYNDA We've all been tired and he's tried to get us more time off. Little signs of consideration which is nice because it makes us want to work harder and give him more instead of moaning.

So deliberate attempts at fostering cohesion had already been made in the short break between *Columba* and the tour. The ritual enacting of 'We-ness' in this first, purely dance, performance had consolidated the renewed experience of being a group. But the particular episode where rapport could be publicly heard in a specific, unrehearsed intonation, was seized on as the tangible evidence of a new and heightened rapport. It was regarded as a somewhat mysterious event and was talked about. In Laing's terminology, it was a demonstration of the 'extraordinary being formed by each person's synthesis of the same multiplicity into We, and each person's syntheses of the multiplicity of syntheses'.

'I feel it's a group, rather than two or three or one.'

It is apparent that this experience of group rapport is confined to the dancers and extended to include Stuart. It arises powerfully from the nature of the task. Gavin, Lisa and Geoffrey, though members of the group, do not show themselves before an audience in what I have termed the ritualised public performance of 'We-ness'. Their work task is an individual contribution. They belong, as asserted, but their experience of belonging differs from the dancers' experience of belonging.

Before leaving considerations of membership I have to reflect on my own role in relation to the group. Was I, in any sense, a member of *Movable Workshop?* Is there a place where I should be slotted into the diagram? In formal legal terms, obviously not. I had no contract with the company: the funds for the research came from another source. I was a non-participant observer contributing nothing to the classes, rehearsals, workshops and performances. For practical reasons, and to assist the detachment necessary to research, I deliberately did not attempt full scale coverage of events. I selected activities, appeared at those, then withdrew. In order to understand the experience of being on tour, I travelled for three days with the company. Apart from this, however, I visited them in various regions for a day at a time only. Yet it would be specious to claim only a fluctuating and impersonal role. I had a task which in the face to face situation appeared to be that of watcher and listener. My long term responsibilities as researcher were less apparent. As watcher and listener, I was in a relationship with individuals, pairs, trios, the entire group. One child, intrigued by my puzzling presence at a school dinner table, leaned over to Peter and asked, 'Is that your head lady?' Peter looked round at the other dancers, was entertained at the ambiguity of the phrase, and replied, 'Yes, she's our head lady.' The pun which the dancers intended in assenting to this was an association with 'head shrinker', but whatever I was, I was theirs. When I sat watching a performance, the 'We-ness' which I was very powerfully conscious of was a 'We-ness' with *Movable Workshop* not with the teachers in the audience with whom, in age and professional training, I had theoretically stronger affinities. These previous associations had been over-ridden by my feeling of association with a new group.

I have attempted this analysis because the role of researcher poses problems which cannot be resolved by a pretence that the researcher does not exist:

The tradition of empirical psychology has denied the subjective to the point where adherents communicate among themselves as though we could have research without researchers and thinking without thinkers. (Pym, 1974, p. 224).

As Rowan (1974, pp. 76, 97) has asserted in the same collection of readings, *Reconstructing Social Psychology:*

Psychology is essentially a reflexive science: that is, the findings of the psychologist about his subjects must also apply in some way to the psychologist himself and his own activities.

This is true even of the so called 'clean' laboratory situation, as Rowan (1974) points out in his comments on the work of Orne:

It seemed clear that the experimental situation which had been treated for all these years as a purely rational and 'clean' situation where accurate observations could be made free from bias was actually a highly potent social field with very strong forces at work . . .

But the basic problem remains: the university psychological laboratory is a highly authority-structured situation in which the experimenter has very high social status. This may be the last thing which the experimenter wants, but he has it, whether he wants it or not. The point is that the experimenter can vary the effect which he has, but not do away with it.

If this is true of the laboratory situation, then it must be even more true of a prolonged field situation. My queries about my own membership are a recognition of the inevitable interaction between researcher and those being researched. The members of the company affected me: their comments, opinions and values entered into my experience: their acceptance of my presence affected my self-image. I must reciprocally have had an effect on them in spite of a scrupulous restraint from any form of direct counselling or manipulation. Indeed it is possible that the consciousness of being a group and the sense of possessing some form of group identity, though arising from more fundamental sources, may have been strengthened by the mere knowledge that the research was concerned with 'group dynamics'. If having a wardrobe mistress can reinforce your group identity, so can having a researcher. My listening may have legitimised the expression of feeling, encouraging an openness and readiness to communicate which was one of the group's characteristics as commented on by teachers and lecturers in the institutions visited. My acknowledgement of these possible additional influences strengthens rather than undermines the analyses offered in this and earlier chapters, since it faces rather than denies the reflexive character of the research operation.

So group membership is a complex concept built up of many layers of meaning. The simplest way to define it is at the formal, legal level of registers, contracts, salary lists etc. It is possible to belong in the formal sense, however, without belonging in the sentient sense. Thus if part of the membership operates in face to face interaction, and part not, it is easy for the latter to feel only a technical membership. Where sentient belonging also operates, it is still possible for this to function at a low level, with the concept of group little more than a reification, and little evidence of any merging of individuality into the larger collectivity. I have suggested that this merging is more likely to occur where the very nature of the group task demands not an aggregation of individual efforts, but sensitive interaction. I suggest further that this collective sensitivity is essential for any group where the task demands improvisation within a set framework. There is evidence that the individuals comprising *Movable Workshop* achieved both formal and high level sentient membership, and that on occasions the dancers experienced a further dimension of group rapport. As for the researcher, I hope that an admission of some level of sentient membership of the group will strengthen rather than invalidate the objectivity of this account.

6

WHAT SORT OF GROUP?

Three approaches to analysis

The evidence reveals that members of *Movable Workshop* felt a sense of cohesion, of belonging to the group, but what sort of group was it to which they belonged? So far no analysis has been offered. Groups have been categorised according to a range of variables. Thus size has been taken as a key variable, and monads, dyads and triads have been investigated by Simmel (1925) von Weise and Becker (1932) and later experimenters. The type of social interaction, from small scale intimate to large scale impersonal, has been used as the criterion of difference by, for instance Tönnies and Loomis (1940). Range of interests combined with degrees of organisation have been utilised by MacIver and Page (1950, pp. 215, 218). The distinction which the latter go on to explore in detail, however, and which encompasses all these earlier perspectives, is the broad one, first postulated by Cooley, between 'the *primary* group, the intimate face to face collectivity' as contrasted with 'the large scale *association*, the great impersonal organisations of man'.

Argyle (1969) has posited five kinds of small social group: 1. the family, 2. adolescent groups, 3. work groups, 4. committees, problem solving and creative groups and 5. T groups and therapy groups. This, of course, is merely a list clustering existing studies and is not offered as a categorisation based on coherent conceptualisation. For another variable we should have to extrapolate the concept of function, and distinguish work groups from social groups. On the evidence already mustered we can then affirm that *Movable Workshop* constitutes a primary group with the function of work.

This, however, does not take us very far. We need to know what characterises primary groups. We need to refine the broad categorisations in order to pin point the special characteristics which distinguish this particular primary workgroup from other possible types of primary workgroups. In this chapter I shall offer as evidence the description of one working day on tour. To this description I shall apply several modes of analysis, supplementing the basic evidence with material drawn from other occasions. It is customary to utilise a single explanatory model in relation to evidence. I intend to go beyond this. By utilising three different ways of interpreting the group's experience I can provide a richer, more satisfying answer to the question.

* * * * * *

A brisk February morning, sparkling light and a nip in the air. I have driven some sixty miles, and find the school in an attractive setting on the outskirts of a small town. The site is established meadow and parkland: beyond the skeleton trees the hills undulate to open country. The building is low and unobtrusive, modern in design and revealing on closer view that faint shabbiness which rapidly afflicts contemporary materials. I know the company have already arrived because, parked alongside the side entrance to the kitchens, is the minibus and the hulking van. I find the main entrance. The school is well equipped with two gymnasia, games hall and language laboratories. Nowhere in its corridors do I see flowers, plants, art work, prints, displays of any kind. A polished oak board shows the inscribed names of the captains of the school and those who have distinguished themselves in the examinations . . .

In the hall the company were already at work. Gavin was dealing with the lights and sound equipment, Marita and Gary were on stage in leotards, Stuart down in the body of the hall wearing his director's working gear of black pants and sweater. Stuart broke off the rehearsal to tell me that the company was very much under strength. Geoffrey was ill with gastro-enteritis and Bob had had to take over the driving of the minibus in order to get them to the school. Fionna had also succumbed and the doctor had said she must take a week off. The entire performance was therefore having to be revised to cover for her absence. I had walked in at the point where *Caritas* was being rehearsed. This dance, an exploration of love and lust, provided a dramatic finale to the whole performance and was usually danced by Lynda, Gary, Fionna and Peter. Now Marita was learning Fionna's part before the afternoon session. Stuart's public manner was calm and reassuring. He pointed out details that were still not quite right, demonstrated moves, called in the other dancers to mark out sections. Modifications were needed in a number of other items also. The whole programme had to be re-structured which entailed Gavin changing the sequence of lighting and sound, Bob adapting the music. Everyone in the group worked with a subdued intensity. Gary was very pale. The strong planes of his mid-western face were almost cadaverous, his eyes hollowed, and I discovered that he too was feeling ill. There was no protest at the demands being made; no complaints of their impossibility. By lunch time the necessary adaptations had been gone through. Stuart had been able to seize a few moments to talk to me. The visit to the previous school had been very demanding. No one seemed to know what the company was there for, the staff seemed quite unprepared, and the children had been restless and difficult to hold. The aftermath was a lot of self-doubt and questioning: were the demands being made and the effort required really justified? All this to me, in snatches. Publicly, he smiled encouragement.

Lunch did nothing to raise the spirits. We queued for a cafeteria meal; no staff joined us or seemed to eat with the children. The dancers, with a performance ahead, chose salad. They said that often they had to forego the main part of a school dinner as it was too stodgy and fattening for them to be able to perform afterwards. Peter was sitting next to a young coloured boy of about twelve. The boy asked him what his work was. Peter said, 'I'm a dancer.' The boy said 'Yes, I know. But what's your work?' Peter persisted. 'But your real work?' Peter repeated that dance was his real work. The boy wrestled with this new idea, then grinned. 'You mean you get paid. I think I'll be a dancer then. It's a nice easy life.'

After lunch we went to the assistant rector's room which had been handed over as a dressing room. Lisa, who had been adjusting Fionna's costumes for Marita, was ironing. Lynda took off the shoes she had worn at lunch and began painting her feet with antiseptic. I looked at the upturned sole of one foot and was horrified. It was lacerated with unhealed splits and bleeding raw spots. The other was the same, and I exclaimed as I saw them. As modern dancers the company of course performed barefoot and I wondered how she could continue. Lynda dabbed at the raw places imperturbably. She said that many of the surfaces they danced on were quite unsuitable—hall floors or stages that were too slippy or were worn and uneven. Some were half swept and dirty. Two days earlier she had danced on a drawing pin and it had been several seconds and many steps later before she could pull it out. I winced at her feet, as a lay person horrified. Gary came over and looked down at them. He said, 'They're like stigmata, aren't they?'

Gary and Peter admitted that so far on the tour they had been disappointed by the fact that though the audiences for the performances were almost always mixed, the schools usually provided a group of girls for the workshop sessions.

'What's the point?' said Gary, 'Little girls like ballet in any case. It makes me mad when they just give us workshops with the girls. It's so narrow-minded. It makes what we are trying to do impossible.' Lynda joined in. She quoted a man teacher from a previous school who had said, 'You see, we have this tradition that Scottish men are strong, virile and not soft.' One of his women colleagues had added, 'Yes, and that's how we like them. It sounds as if you are trying to change our culture.' Everyone in the group, hearing Lynda recount this, made 'Yuk, Yuk' sounds of disgust, but Gary and Peter expressed their indignation more seriously. 'If a culture doesn't change it dies', said Gary.

Stuart said that he would try to get some boys allocated to the afternoon workshop. He slipped out in order to talk to the Principal Teacher in Physical Education about the afternoon's arrangements. When he was out there was some rueful griping. Lisa said that dirty stages wrecked the costumes and made washing a nightmare. Marita said how difficult it was to change, remove make up etc when the schools passed over the children for the workshops almost immediately after the performance, thus cutting down the length of the break.

I went into the hall before the performance and sat next to a primary teacher. She said that her school had received an invitation to bring a group of children and that most of her ten year old class had come. She had no idea what was in store and asked if they were going to see a full length ballet. Beside me were some girls from the secondary school itself. They told me that the audience were all volunteers; the three of them had been to ballet classes when younger and were now taking music, so they had wanted to come. The audience was predominantly female, with a scattering of boys.

The performance started. Stuart was on stage, dressed in the formal grey suit which he wore to give his spoken commentary and which, although akin to the teachers' suits, was very much 'costume' to him and the dancers—meticulously hung and brushed between performances. His commentary seemed a little flatter than usual. The dancers started on their preliminary sketches.

Dance by Addition was rather slipshod, the humour coming over broadly and with less crispness. But when the dancers came off stage to mingle with the audience and greet individuals, they managed a front of smiling friendliness and apparent spontaneity. This sudden descent from stage always surprised and delighted audiences, shaking them out of their preconceptions as to appropriate behaviour for performers and spectators. Bob was accustomed to follow this up with a rhythm section in which the audience provided the sounds to which the dancers improvised. This afternoon, without warning, he divided the audience differently, directing some sections from the sides. This led to a considerable dispersal of interest with Bob being compelled to run round three sides instead of directing operations from the front. Again the dancers reacted by broadening the humour, but this unsubtle approach began to work. The children were warming to the group, were laughing in the right places. In *Charade,* a costume piece, they quietened, responding to the mimed pathos; theatrically this work came over. Gary who up to now had been only semi-committed, conserving his energies by dancing with an almost throw away casualness, began to intensify his performance, responding to the rising enthusiasm. Peter projected well throughout. Marita carried off Fionna's sections in addition to her own roles, ultimately excelling herself in *Caritas.* She gave the dance a different quality from Fionna's version, but no-one would have guessed that she had just learned the part. The performance ended with tumultuous applause. A teacher rose to say that those pupils who did Scottish country dancing and belonged to the drama group could stay for the workshop: the rest were to go. There were groans of disappointment from the children who had to leave.

I slipped round to the assistant rector's room, where the dancers were returning for a tea break. Stuart embraced Marita and the rest crowded round to congratulate her. There was a generous exchange of praise—everyone delighted that the performance had gone so unexpectedly well. The dancers removed stage make up and got into their workshop clothes. The girls wore black leotards with sweaters which could later be stripped off as they got into action. Bob, Gary and Peter wore jeans with a motley collection of T-shirts—Peter's with Mickey Mouse printed across it.

The tea break was brief—less than twenty minutes. Stuart had heard that the workshop group would be large. Frequently in such circumstances he sub-divided into two, but since these pupils were likely to be inexperienced in dance he decided to keep them together so that he could utilise music and percussion from Bob. He told this to the others and added that the P.E. master had said he might be able to bring in the rugger team towards the end of the afternoon. Reactions to this were predictably mixed: boys, yes, considerable approval, but a rugger team!

We went to the gym where a group of about eighty girls was waiting, ages twelve upwards. There were too many for the available space. Many of them were dressed in tight skirts which totally restricted movement, knee length white socks which would soil or fall down. They were excited but apprehensive. Stuart, in black jump suit, carried a small drum. He quickly got the girls organised, allowing them to move freely initially, but, because of congestion, rapidly progressing to a sequence to be done in lines. This was a sequence of stride, balance, jump, stretch, hop and spin. The dancers distributed themselves, working directly with the children, stimulating them with smiles and verbal encouragement, setting a standard of performance by actually doing the sequences alongside them. The girls moved clumsily, some restricted and inhibited, others, yielding to exuberance, lurching and uncontrolled. Yet, as the session developed, all looked more animated, more alert and revitalised. Bob, using percussion, stepped up the rhythm and a sense of speed and liveliness was generated. Stuart was the central source of energy, demonstrating, giving coaching points, controlling numbers, directing Bob, the dancers, the pupils. Gary, who had looked about to faint at one point, sat quietly on a bench at the side for the last ten minutes. His withdrawal was noticed by the other dancers, who redistributed themselves in relation to the children, encouraging, demonstrating with tremendous commitment. Towards the end Stuart subdivided the pupils to work on shapes in groups: as a finale to make a centre group. The numbers involved in this centre mass looked terrifying; using a flute to slow the mood, he caused them to scatter away, and then re-coalesce in a more sensitive and controlled fashion. The class was then dismissed in a mood of restrained exuberance.

There was time for only a quick word on strategy before the Rugby team appeared. 'We'll start with floor work', said Stuart. 'We've just got to work them hard at the start.' Then, clad in Rugby shirts and shorts, the fifteen year olds clumped in. Huge, resentful and sheepish, they towered above the girl dancers. Their presence was spotted by some of the departing pupils, who lingered at the doors and even moved round to peer, giggling, through the windows. Stuart began. He demonstrated at floor level a back arching exercise which he and the dancers performed with great flexibility but which the boys found very difficult since it was outside their range of training. He asked the dancers to go round coaching, and quite matter-of-factly Marita and Lynda slipped hands under spines, pushed down knees etc. Stuart kept up a great pace, explaining, demonstrating, speaking from very difficult postures, the whole designed to show these lads the breath control, flexibility and strength of the dancer's body though not, of course, in so many words. His manner was pleasant, direct, unemphatic—of course dancers need flexible torsoes, strong leg muscles, etc. The boys sweated at the floor exercises, striving to co-operate, locked and muscle bound, groaning with exertion. After this demonstration of effortless superiority which had been accompanied by no hint of superiority in tone but an invariable quiet courtesy, the boys were divided into rows, a dancer with each. Then they practised a sequence of 'stride, leap, roll and stand. Their elevation was extremely good but timing and control poor. They thundered in ranks down the room, sweating and labouring, now fully involved but mis-timing and lumbering.

The dancers sped with them. The cool, friendly yet businesslike way in which Marita and Lynda had coped had robbed the situation of any sexual frisson—the giggling girls had left the windows and doors. The final movements of the workshop, though dance-like, had been chosen for their relevance to Rugby and consisted of leg swings, rolls and leaps. Again the boys showed strength and energy, but lack of fine control and swift adjustment. After coaching these points, Stuart dismissed a group who, amiable and sweating, looked very different from the sheepish and bewildered team who had entered half an hour earlier.

The Principal Teacher in Physical Education had been watching from the side with a man and woman colleague. Stuart came over to chat with them. They had been intrigued by the afternoon and thought the sessions had gone well. Dance training had a point—the leap up from a tackle was often too slow. Stuart provided instances of the relevance of dance training to sport—Italian hurdlers, Russian athletes all utilised elements. In this conversation, dance was subordinated to sport, and Stuart held back at this point from putting forward over-strongly claims for the experience in its own right. This tactful self-restraint ensured that the brief discussion could be positive and warm, strengthening the interest already being tentatively manifested.

After that, the hampers were packed, the van loaded and the company drove off. That night they would stay in a different hotel, next day arrive at another school, at 10 a.m. start their own class, at 11 a.m. try out the stage and plan the programme, at 12.30 school lunch. And so on for ten weeks.

THREE APPROACHES TO ANALYSIS

I   The Primary Group

What can be deduced about the nature of the group from this account of one working day? Was behaviour on this day typical? How does this behaviour relate to evidence drawn from studies involving other work contexts? How far does it exemplify concepts applied to a variety of small group situations? To answer these questions I shall relate aspects of this descriptive material to appropriate theoretical concepts, starting with the broad basic concept of 'the primary group.'

> The face to face group is the nucleus of all organisation and, as we shall see, is found in some form within the most complex systems—it is the unit cell of the social structure (MacIver & Page, 1950, p. 219).

Within the formal structure of factories and organisations humans will spontaneously coalesce into primary groups, and the presence of these informal face to face groups and the role they play in production efficiency, workers' 'morale', union activity and the like, have become major considerations to the growing field of 'industrial sociology'. Now *Movable Workshop* was not a spontaneous grouping within a larger organisation. For all members apart from Stuart and Geoffrey, the link with the main company was too tenuous to be felt as a reality. *Movable Workshop* was itself the formal organisation and its members did not coalesce spontaneously but were officially recruited. Yet by the criteria postulated by MacIver and Page (1950, pp. 224-5), drawn from an overview of the relevant literature, the company constituted a primary group:

> In primary group life our relations with others are always, to some extent, *personal*.

This in contrast to the 'categoric' relations in large organisations where people confront each other in specialised roles. This quality of relationship can usually only be achieved in a group of limited *size,* where members share a *similarity of background*. A further characteristic of primary group life is *limited self-interest*.

> The common interest must be strong enough to control the inevitable self-assertive impulses which are exhibited in all face to face association . . . Under the conditions just described, any interest becomes focused and enriched in the group process.

Each is spurred on in his pursuit by the fact that others are
pursuing with him. When his own energy and devotion flag . . .
he is sustained by the energy and devotion of his fellows.

The appropriateness of this survey of the characteristics of
primary groups to *Movable Workshop* will be immediately
apparent. Size? Only ten members. Relationships? Personal
rather than categoric. Similarity of background? As far as
nationality, members came from very different locations,
Marita being Australian, Gary American, Geoffrey Irish,
Fionna, Gavin and Lisa Scottish, and the remaining four
English. All were young, however, Stuart at thirty-one being
the oldest, and more important, every member had one
attribute in common which was powerful enough to override
all differences; namely, an enthusiasm for dance and for the
theatre arts. As for the characteristic of limited self interest,
my account of one day's work demonstrates the participant,
co-operative spirit which modifies self-assertive impulses in
primary groups. The flexibility and adaptability of members
in restructuring the programme, in covering without any
public acknowledgment for the absence of others, their praise
of each other's achievements, shows a subordination of
personal demands to the implementation of the group's goals.
And the power of the group to stimulate flagging enthusiasm
and to energise its members is brought out in my recognition
of the growing commitment and increasing dynamism in
performance and workshops on that day. As Peter and Fionna
asserted on another occasion in discussion:

PETER We work together as friends, not as workers.

　　　'Or as rivals?'

PETER No, not at all. We *don't* work as rivals.
FIONNA No. I'm not conscious of anybody trying to be over
　　　anyone else. It's just us and the audience.
PETER Us *together* and the audience.

My observations of *Movable Workshop* on tour and their own comments demonstrate that an organisation, if it is small enough, can manifest the characteristics of the spontaneous primary group.

II   Amateur and Professional

There is another quite different analytical concept which can be applied to *Movable Workshop,* the concept of 'professional' versus 'amateur'. The word 'professional' when used in polarity with 'amateur' has little to do with the 'professions' as such. Professions have been a focal point of sociological study ever since Marx attempted to establish the secondary and derivative character of professional classes particularly in terms of their negative contribution to surplus value, and Durkheim asserted that, with the disturbance of the established moral order brought about by division of labour, professional organisations were sources of consensus and ought to become 'so many moral milieux'. More recent studies of the professions have listed 'traits' by means of which occupations can be categorised as 'professional' or 'semi professional', or have posited functionalist models. Thus Parsons (1968) sees professions as the embodiment of the 'primacy of cognitive rationality' and Barber (1963) sees professional behaviour as oriented to community interest rather than self interest, society rewarding such highly valued performance by means of money and prestige.[1] The weaknesses of both the trait and functionalist approaches have been exposed by Rueschemeyer (1964), and, more comprehensively, by Johnson (1972). Johnson offers an alternative analysis in which the management of the relationship between producer and client is the key factor.

[1] See Marx, K., *Theories of Surplus Value* (Vol. IV of *Capital*) trans. Emile Burns. . . . . . .: Lawrence & Wishart Ltd, 1969, part I, Chap. IV; Durkheim, E., *Professional Ethics and Civic Morals* trans. C. Brookfield. New York: Routledge & Kegan Paul, 1957, p. 29; Millerson, G., *The Qualifying Associations: A Study in Professionalisation.* New York: Routledge & Kegan Paul, 1964; Parsons, T., Professions. In *The International Encyclopaedia of the Social Sciences.* New York, 1968, p. 539; Barber, B., Some problems in the sociology of the professions. *Daedalus,* 1963, 671-2.

Where an occupational group has the resources of power to impose its own definitions of the producer-consumer relationship, to define the needs of the consumer and the manner in which those needs shall be met, then this is described by Johnson (1972, pp. 45, 51), as collegiate control:

> A profession is not then an occupation, but a means of controlling an occupation, (and 'professionalism' is the ideology of this type of control). 'Professionalism' arises where the tensions inherent in the producer-consumer relationship are controlled by means of an institutional framework based on occupational authority.

Where clients are specially vulnerable as when sick or entangled in the law, the relationship between producer and client is very open to exploitation and institutionalised forms of control are very necessary. 'Professionalism', then, is redefined by Johnson as a peculiar type of occupational control rather than an expression of the inherent nature of particular occupations. Two other forms of control of producer-client relationships are indicated by Johnson. Thus the client or consumer can have sufficient power to define his own needs and the manner in which they are to be met. This constitutes 'patronage', either oligarchic or corporate. Or there may be 'mediative' control, in which the capitalist entrepreneur or the state mediate between producer and consumer in the definition of needs and ways in which they shall be satisfied. The professions and semi-professions, as conventionally understood, exemplify or strive towards 'collegiate' control, but are increasingly being subjected to the latter two forms.

What, if anything, of this applies to the use of 'professional' in the specific fields of sports and the arts? Under the old 'trait' theory of the professions, specific elements such as length of training, mastery of specialised knowledge could be extrapolated and hopefully applied: this because trait theory is so imprecise that it fits a range of occupations very little worse than its fits the so called 'learned professions'. But the key element in the professions is not a set of characteristics manifested by the occupation or its practitioners, but a special inter-relationship with the power structures of society, and it is here that Johnson's analysis is more fruitful. In terms of inter-relationships with power structures, then dance companies, operatic societies, drama groups, games teams and athletes have nothing in common with doctors, lawyers, architects and bishops. They cannot impose their own definitions of the producer-client relationship by means of collegiate control: indeed, it is not always easy to assert who *are* the clients of a dance company, an actors' group, a games team. The spectators, yes! But between producer and spectator may come the oligarchical control of the individual or corporate patron or the mediative control of entrepeneur or state, imposing their definition of needs on the producers/dancers/actors/athletes and becoming in a very real sense themselves the clients.

So although 'professional' as adjective or noun is used in both the contexts of 'the learned professions' and the contexts of sports and the arts, its employment in the latter differs profoundly from its employment in the former. The best way to discern its significance for the dance group is therefore to examine the usage of the term by members themselves.

The basic use of 'professional' as noun is to indicate someone who is paid, whose full-time employment consists of the specific activity: as adjective, performed for payment. Because participation in sport and the arts can be a highly self-gratifying occupation many people indulge without payment as 'amateurs', for love and no cash. Hence the dichotomy. So Gary says in the early days of rehearsing in Glasgow:

> We're professionals in that we are being paid, but this is new to all of us. Perhaps in another month or so we'll get used to the idea. Still seems funny that all we've to do is dance all day and we get a salary. I've danced all day for quite a while and no-one has given me a salary.

Larry asserts:

> I've done more than the others in a professional kind
> of way. Been on the stage and been paid for it.

The salary is part of a contractual transaction and makes
possible membership of a union. As Gavin says of his stage-
managing:

> I've done it all before. But in a purely amateur sense.
> This gets me into Equity.

Sport is a competitive activity and there is a strong likelihood
that those who earn a living at it and therefore train full-time
will have the advantage over the part-timer. Because of the
competitive element and because of the powerful interests,
both financial and national, vested in the process of winning,
rules defining the 'amateur' as against the 'professional'
have proliferated since 1867 (British Amateur Athletic
Association) and 1894 (Olympic formulation), and have been
heavily coloured with class significance. In the arts the
distinction between amateur and professional has been less
regulated, although obviously to the unions the issue is
becoming of increasing importance.

Once an undertaking becomes a job rather than a hobby,
then it acquires the characteristics of 'work': Gary sees these
as protective and advantageous rather than burdensome:

GARY I feel we work very hard but it isn't a strain.

> 'What takes the strain out of it?'

GARY It's the salary, having a place to go, and it's a job. I
get up in the morning, go to work at 10 o'clock and
come back at six and I can just leave it then and forget
it and go the next day and do it again. So I feel very
objective about it. When I'm there I work as hard as I
can and then come home and drop it just like any

other job and it's very refreshing. You see, Stuart will never call us at seven or nine in the evening to start rehearsing because that's the rules for the job. It starts and ends at this time and we get paid overtime and it's very efficient. Stuart is very professional and its all on a very objective level and it makes it very easy to work.

'What do you mean by very professional?'

GARY When we are rehearsing that's all there is. Just the rehearsal, just the dance and nothing else is brought in—nothing from outside into rehearsal except the dance, working on the dance and then going as far as you can, then forgetting it until you come back to it—keeping it very objective.

'You talk as if you have had experiences that were very different.'

GARY Yes. You see this New Mountain Dance Company that I was with—three of the people were friends of mine and we had known each other for four years and that whole four years was brought into every rehearsal. All kinds of resentments we'd built up over the four years.

'I wonder what you'll feel like a year from now.'

GARY Yes, that's a good point.

Of course, as time went on, inevitably there seeped into the rehearsals something more than the dance, emotions from outside, some of them hostile. Nevertheless, in pinpointing this concentration on work goals as the sign of professionalism, and recognising that a work task is regulated by rules for the protection of workers, Gary is making important distinctions.

But to be a professional goes beyond drawing a salary and a union card and performing in work-oriented and regulated conditions. It imposes certain ways of behaving which are asserted as the norms of professionalism:

STUART   We are not running a therapy group. We are running a professional company and we must behave as professionals and if you find a thing difficult you must make the best of it.

MARITA   Lynda is really quite a calm and composed person—really very professional.

Composure, equanimity, persistence and resilience in difficulties are the valued characteristics. Just because so much is unpredictable in terms of physical conditions of work, just because, in a public and scheduled group activity, absence can create acute problems, just because audience response can be bizarre and unexpected, then certain qualities which can be depended on in crisis become the attributes of 'professionalism'. Sometimes these manifestations of 'professionalism' can be a tiresome front, part of the self-display of the old hand:

MARITA   With professionalism you do get such an air of confidence—everyone being a little bit over-confident though very often they're not, and this can come out in a very nasty form and make a very unhappy company.

Members of *Movable Workshop* are not professionalised in this case-hardened sense:

Whereas there is quite a lot of give and take in this company which I think is marvellous.

Though a freshness and spontaneity remains, individuals are acquiring insight into and internalisation of the norms of 'professionalism'. The responsibility to colleagues to make the work task feasible even in difficult conditions is supplemented by a responsibility to the clients/spectators expressed in the cliché, 'The show must go on.' Garry, halfway through the tour, gives the most lengthy exposition of these desirable attributes of professionalism in relation to Marita:

FIONNA We've all got our places in the van.

GARY I always sit in the back seat.

FIONNA Yes, and Marita always sits behind Stuart and Geoffrey—like the binding link—tolerant.

GARY Yes—she's so professional—the most professional person amongst us.

'Do you feel more professional yourselves?'

GARY It's funny. I feel like I know *how* to be more professional but I can't always apply it in the situation.

'You seem able to recognise it.'

GARY Yes. I feel we are very professional in a way because of the amazing conditions—I mean, we danced on that stage last night. But at the same time I feel we're not the kind of professionals Geoffrey and Stuart talk about when they say 'That's not a very professional attitude you're taking.' Then I don't understand what it is at all. But Marita is a professional because for her this show must go on sort of thing. She just gets right down to work. There's something to be done so she does it—goes on stage and does the best she can. She's covered for us in bad situations. She covered for Fionna, and when I hurt my foot she went on in *Uneven Time* which is almost impossible to teach—she did it in about fifteen minutes—charged in and was great. I sat in the audience and watched our show. I was really proud of us and our show. Because it was such a difficult situation to be in and Stuart

took over from me and Marita danced and it was
really good.

The skill, versatility and commitment that ensure that the
show will go on are means of protecting the client/spectators'
interests, and through these the interests of the pro-
ducer/dancers. If spectators never knew whether a
performance would ensue then the whole 'professional
theatre' would collapse. Thus 'the show must go on' is not a
generous manifestation of warm hearted artistry, though it
can take on that coloration, but a harsh economic necessity.
Because it calls into play stamina, resilience and technical
expertise, it gives rise to a warm pride that Gary's account
vividly communicates. The internalisation of the values
implicit in the cliché is a 'professional' necessity for
newcomers to the field.

The usage of the term 'professional' by members of
Movable Workshop showed that it applied to skilled,
appropriate behaviour, but one aspect of that behaviour was
so taken for granted that they themselves never singled it out.
Nevertheless, it was sufficiently striking for me to have
already called attention to it in my earlier description of one
day's proceedings.

One aspect of a skilled occupational performance is that it
should support an appropriate definition of the reality of an
interaction situation. In certain situations, this definition of
reality is relatively precarious. Thus doctors must provide a
setting and manifest behaviours that induce in the patient the
conviction that 'this is a medical situation' not, as Emerson
(1970, p. 78) has expressed it:

> ... not a party, sexual assault, psychological experiment, or
> anything else. If it is a medical situation, then it follows that 'no
> one is embarrassed' and no one is thinking in sexual terms.

Although far less extreme than a medical situation,
nevertheless in dance training a wider range of touch and
body contact is legitimised than in many teaching situations.
Therefore an essential element of 'professional' performance

in workshops is the appropriate setting, the dress which signals the fact that this is a dance session, and an assured performance from the staff. To quote Emerson again from the medical situation:

> The scene is credible precisely because the staff acts as if they have every right to do what they are doing.

When *Movable Workshop* members undertook a dance session with a Rugby team, they involved in the interaction process individuals who had clear concepts of the kinds of reality involved in a particular team game, but considerable insecurity as to the nature of the reality of a dance situation. The costume of leotards, tights, sweaters and T-shirts, the bare feet, signalled that this was no ordinary lesson and established the setting, but the boys' clothing signalled something different. Had the performances of the staff lacked assurance, then the social scene would have collapsed in disarray. The giggling girls at doorways and windows were a clear indication that its reality was precarious. It is a tribute to the 'professional' quality of the performance of all the workshop dancers that such a collapse never occurred. Marita, Lynda and the rest produced behaviour of such matter of fact conviction that their definition of the scene as a 'dance training workshop' became the accepted one, in spite of the inexperience of the boys. The girls drifted away.

It perhaps is perverse to end a section where I have been at pains to establish the special use of 'professional' in the context of the theatre arts with an analogy drawn from the 'profession' of medicine. As I have asserted earlier, the special relationship of the learned professions with the power structures of society, which enabled them to develop a particular collegiate control of the producer-client re-lationship, differentiates them from other occupations. Nevertheless, in these other occupations people may manifest 'professional', that is, skilled and appropriate performances. To sum up, in sporting and artistic contexts the term 'professional' denotes basically the person who is paid. On this dichotomy between amateur and professional an expectation of particular attitudes and behaviours is raised. The evidence mustered so far throws some light on these in relation to dance and the performing arts.

It is possible to assert, therefore, in answer to the question 'What sort of a Group?', that *Movable Workshop* constituted a primary work group whose members were professionals in that they were paid for their full time labour. More subtly, they were 'professionals' in that, during the course of the tour, they were acquiring and demonstrating those norms of behaviour which they themselves understood as 'professional'.

III   The Dramaturgical Model

This does not exhaust the analysis of 'what sort of group?' It will not have escaped attention that although my aim was to illuminate 'professionalism' the Goffman inter-actionist model underlies some of my comments on the company's afternoon workshop with the group of boys. I wish now to make this model explicit by applying Goffman's concept of the 'performance team' to the dance group.

Goffman (1959) in *The Presentation of the Self in Everyday Life,* propounds a dramaturgical model of social interaction, seeing it as a quasi-theatrical performance in which the individual presents his version of the reality of a situation by means of a chosen setting, appearance, posture, gesture, words, a range of non-verbal and verbal cues. Impression-management takes place in the 'front' regions of work places and homes when appropriate audiences are present: in the 'back' regions the 'performer can relax: he can drop his front,' forgo speaking his line and step out of character.' Goffman cites such instances as the waiter moving from kitchen to dining room, the hostess moving from the 'back' region of the bedroom to greet visitors in the 'front'. The element of self-consciousness, from good faith to guile, may vary, but social interactions in 'front' regions are necessarily 'performances':

> A status, a position, a social place is not a material thing, to be
> possessed and then displayed: it is a pattern of appropriate
> conduct, coherent, embellished and well-articulated. Performed

with ease or clumsiness, awareness or not, guile or good faith, it is none the less something that must be enacted and portrayed, something that must be realised (Goffman, 1959, p. 75).

Goffman has posited, in addition to the individual performer, the concept of:

> ... the performance team, any set of individuals who co-operate in staging a single routine.
>
> It may even be said that if our special interest is the study of impression management, of the contingencies which arise in fostering an impression, and of the techniques for meeting these contingencies, then the team and the team performance may well be the best units to take as the fundamental point of reference (Goffman, 1959, pp. 79-80).

Argyle (1972, p. 104) has commented severely on this dramaturgical model, asserting that it:

> ... applies quite well to confidence men, has some application to some aspects of professional performances, and very little application to everyday life.

(Note, incidentally, the ambiguity of the use of 'professional'; does it mean performances given, say, by a doctor performing as a member of a profession, an actor/sportsman performing as a 'professional', or anyone performing an occupational role effectively?) This reaction seems to me to over-emphasise the role of conscious guile in the dramaturgical model and to be tinged with a degree of moral disapproval. I think that while the model is only *one* metaphor to illumine human interaction, it is nevertheless a sharp, wry, probing and entertaining one. We recognise with rueful acknowledgment the personal applicability in everyday life of many of Goffman's instances.

The problem of applying this concept of a 'performance team' to *Movable Workshop* is that, in a strictly *non*-metaphorical sense, they *were* a performance team in that they staged performances for audiences. There is obviously a danger of ambiguity when a quasi-theatrical image is applied to a genuinely theatrical group. To reduce this, I shall leave out of consideration their actual staged performances.

It will be apparent even from my earlier description of a single working day that the company functioned as a 'performance team' in the Goffman sense. In the back region—on this day the assistant rector's room—they slumped, dispirited and griping; Lynda attended to her feet, Gary discussed his symptoms, all expressed apprehension at covering for missing members. Lisa doggedly tackled the endless washing and ironing which enabled the group to sustain their 'front' image. Teachers were, by implication, criticised for offering only girls at the workshops: directly, the reported comments of two teachers were greeted by derisory expressions of disgust. Strategy was planned, and Stuart left to implement it. In this back region the performers relaxed, dropped their front. The 'back region' is not, however, confined to a physical place, though a place offers tangible shelter to performers temporarily shedding roles. Stuart swiftly re-created the 'back region' in the gym after the girls had left and before the boys had entered. In the temporary absence of an audience, strategy for sustaining the reality of the next performance was swiftly gone through—a 'back region' verbal activity perforce taking place in a 'front' space.

In 'front', the team interacted consistently to sustain the version of reality that this was a dance group. Their feet ceased killing them, and they walked into school dining halls, into hotel foyers, with none of the limps, groans and winces they permitted themselves in private. The illusion of bodies in perfect fitness, alertly sensitive to any aesthetic demand, was sustained not only on stage but in workshops and public places. At the point where Gary was forced by illness to drop out, he did it unobtrusively. The others showed no concern: to have done so would have been to draw attention to something that would splinter the illusion. In interaction with teachers, where differences of viewpoint occurred, these were handled with honest but tactful and smiling argument: any expressions of disgust being saved, presumably by both parties, for the privacy of staffrooms and other back regions.

In the workshops, the special gear, the percussion and other instruments, and the consistency of all performers ensured that the reality that this was a dance workshop should prevail even with an audience of youths inexperienced in *their* parts and not dressed for this type of interaction. In some situations *Movable Workshop* undoubtedly operated not only as a team of performers in a non-metaphorical sense, but as a 'performance team' on the Goffman dramaturgical model.

So 'what sort of group?' can be answered from no single model but must be refracted through a variety of concepts. To express the answer as succinctly as possible, *Movable Workshop* can be classed as a micro-organisation manifesting all the characteristics of a primary work group, absorbing and enacting the norms of a professional dance company and operating in certain social interactions as a 'performance team'.

7

THE ECOLOGY OF THE GROUP

Problems of Proximity

The minibus is clearly marked territory: 'Dancers of the
Scottish Theatre Ballet' on stickers at side and rear windows.
I have joined the group at a school in Inverness and we are to
drive to Golspie on the remote coast of Eastern Sutherland
that same evening. As we climb into the van, individuals
make unerringly for their places. Geoffrey is in the driving
seat, Stuart at the front next to him. Behind is Marita. Then
Lynda and Peter, and at the back Fionna and Gary. Each
dancer is surrounded by bags with immediate belongings and
provisions for the journey. Cartons of milk, yoghurt, fruit in
plastic bags impede the narrow space between the seats. I
swarm up and take the vacant seat just behind Marita,
clutching my over-night bag and tape recorder. We drive off
promptly because Geoffrey has planned a route over the
mountains and wants us to see the views before darkness. The
van, being too underpowered and ponderous, is to go by a
more orthodox road. Within a very short time we are in a

wilderness of hills and heather that becomes increasingly dramatic. Marita is complaining with exaggerated pathos that there was no time to shop in Inverness, that she wanted just to look at the place but it's always work then rush away; Geoffrey bullies them into the bus—he and Stuart haven't any sympathy. The others join in the banter—they never get into a shop, never see any place except for school halls. All this is met with rallies from Stuart and Geoffrey who are quick-witted in riposte. The tone is light, amusing, but there is a quiver of real frustration, something genuinely rueful under the pretend pathos. Geoffrey begins to sing extracts from Gilbert & Sullivan to howls of dismay from the others. Again this seems part of a regular act and everyone is amiable, even starting up counter-songs. Gary eats a grapefruit. This capacity for eating them raw like an orange astonishes me. Lynda and Fionna say, 'He's *always* eating them.' As the country grows more bare and austere, Gary says it reminds him of New Mexico. The others laugh. 'He's always wanting it to be New Mexico.' 'He's homesick.' 'Ah! is he homesick?' 'It *can't* look like New Mexico.' 'Well, it does, just exactly.'

Again, under the play acting, is a genuine nostalgia.

Peter leans across to Lynda with a bottle of orange juice:

'Will you put this in your bag?'

Lynda says:

'I'm not your slave.'

There is a cold edge to her voice that shows an irritation more than the request justifies. Geoffrey embarks on a facetious running commentary on the passing scene, abetted by Stuart; 'Just a tantalising glimpse from Macnab's tour of our scenic wonderland.' Then, increasing silences as the effects of physical tiredness overwhelm the febrile humour and individuals slump quietly in their seats. Geoffrey drives doggedly over expanses of moor and wilderness. Then, dropping round a curve of the mountain road, he runs the 'bus into a lay-by designed to provide a viewpoint. The sun is setting over the mountains behind, but far below is a great curve of sea. There is silence, and then, 'Nice one, Geoffrey' calls Lynda, and everyone joins the chorus. We all climb out.

Peter takes photographs; we look back over the route we have come by, the mountains in the half-light—then out and beyond, over the lay-by wall, to the sea and the route we have still to follow. It is dark as we drop down to the narrow line of houses following the curve of the bay at Golspie, so dark we can barely make out the statue of the Duke of Sutherland, set with phallic arrogance on the top-most headland dominating the tiny community. It was to this spot that his tenants were evicted in the clearances to make what living they could from the sea while their lands were given over to the sheep. Now, to this still remote community, comes the unlikely troup of dancers.

All the group stay at the same hotel. The lounge is taken over for a meeting and no other guests have the temerity to intrude. The handful who are also staying appear at dinner. There is no inter-action between these middle aged couples and the exotic young people who present such a cohesive and impenetrable front to outsiders. Even Gavin, the non-dancer, with his dark glasses and shock of black hair and beard looks sufficiently unorthodox to constitute a threat to the conventional. Golspie out of season and by night offers no diversions apart from a walk along the darkened main street or over the sand dunes. The dancers rarely indulge in social drinking, partly from guarding their physique, partly from lack of cash. I am struck by the puritanism of their early-to-bed routine: physical exhaustion is always lurking to overwhelm them by 10 p.m. They are sharing twin bedded rooms, as in most hotels. Lynda and Fionna, Marita and Lisa, constitute the regular pairs. Tonight Gary is sharing with Bob, Peter with Gavin, a minor rearrangement amongst the men.

At the breakfast tables, the same faces. Then in the 'bus for the short trip to the school, all taking exactly the same places. Then the training class in the school hall, virtually indistinguishable from the school hall in Inverness, the school hall in Galashiels, the school hall in Perth. Already I have decided to break away for a solitary walk, but they have a rehearsal following the training class. Then school lunch.

Then a performance. Then a workshop with pupils. Then back to the hotel for tea and to prepare for the evening. The school acts as a community centre and a performance is being given there for an adult audience. Posters have been spotted advertising an election meeting in another hall the same night, and there is gloomy speculation as to the effect of this on what can only be a tiny audience at best. The election features in discussion solely as a rival attraction. But in the school hall some seventy people turn up. Some are pupils who have enjoyed the afternoon performance so much that they have returned for a second viewing. Most are adults: one whom I speak to has travelled forty miles to see the dancers. I sit relaxed; confident after the number of performances I have seen that the show will work. Soon these people, most of whom have never seen modern dance before, are laughing, applauding, participating in the deliberately planned interactions of the first half. The second half goes smoothly, the programme ends to delighted applause; Lisa collects up the costumes, equipment is stowed in the van, the company return to the hotel.

Next day is a travelling day, across Scotland to Fort William. Into the 'bus after breakfast, in the same seats; Gavin, Bob and Lisa making their own way in the van. After a preliminary detour, we drive down the shores of Loch Ness, deserted of tourists, its waters impassive, unbroken by any periscopic neck or undulating torso. Hours of confinement as the bleak magnificence of the Scottish landscape slips by. The routines of banter spark up spasmodically. A picnic lunch on the lochside takes on the quality of a treat. The still wintry sun shines briefly and food is shared out and eaten outside. Individuals scramble over boulders and amongst the scrub for better viewpoints and to take snaps. Then, back into the confines of the'bus. Fort William is reached by early evening. As we drive into the hotel parking ground, the van is spotted. The trio are already here. Fort William is a metropolis, with cinemas. Gary and Fionna decide to see *Jesus Christ Super Star*. Both have seen it before, but a night at the pictures is not to be missed. I arranged to tape record that evening, putting Gary and Fionna in first so that they can still see the film. The recording goes on with individuals after dinner from eight to 10.30. I feel guilty at requesting it, but no-one demurs. Everyone has a single room tonight—unusual privacy.

Next morning, the same faces at the breakfast tables. Then over to the school. Lisa has found a laundrette in the town, has washed the costumes and is now ironing them in the school's domestic science quarters. Marita takes the training class in one of the school gymnasia indistinguishable from the school gymnasia at Inverness, Galashiels, Perth and Golspie. Then two workshops with pupils. Then school lunch. Then a performance. That night, a free evening for the delights of Fort William in late February. Next morning, breakfast and then departure in minibus and van for St Andrews.

Social ecology is concerned not only with direct response to environment but with:

> . . . the general conceptualization of the cosmos associated with specific habitats. Conceived in these terms, *ecological studies* are extended to include modern urban societies; and such studies are concerned with the social relationship of people in relation to the constraints and permissiveness of the urban habitat, and in relation to the environment of industry, its location, the limits it sets to domestic and local relationships . . . (Mitchell, 1968, p. 62).

Whether at Kirkcaldy or Kinross, Alloa or Anstruther, Dunblane or Perth, the environment of *Movable Workshop* was the school hall, the gymnasium, the improvised dressing room, the hotel lounge, hotel bedroom, the minibus and the van. Encapsulated in their vehicles, members moved through a changing landscape which could not impinge; and halted in work locations which were mirror images of the ones left behind. They interacted briefly and intensely with large, undifferentiated groups and moved on. The tight proximity of the work and travel situation extended into total living. Technologically advanced humans are accustomed to a division between work life and domestic and social living. Members of the company worked in an unnatural habitat in that they were deprived of this division. Under the pressures imposed by lack of privacy and constant proximity strains and tensions manifested themselves. We know from a wealth of animal studies that an unnatural habitat breeds tension and aggression: the human animal reacts similarly.[1] Group tensions were held in check by the need for ongoing collaboration and by the warmth of feeling engendered in the less pressurised earlier situations in Glasgow. But irritation and frustration broke out; individuals and pairs sought to escape from a claustrophobic relationship.

Gavin was the most articulate in describing the dilemma:

> The whole set-up, ten people travelling around. I've never been in a situation like it before. Because everyone lives in groups but you move from one to another. But I haven't got another group to move to. I'm stuck twenty-four hours a day with the group I work with. It's horrible. I've never been in this situation before. I've worked at college with a group for half a day—worked with people very closely and been very fond of them but then I'd go to another group with an entirely different set of interests. But now I've only one role to play in one group and its driving me up the wall. It really is. I go away and lock myself in the loo for half an hour just to get away from the others. The problem isn't the people. It's the fact that we are touring and we're not in one place long enough to make friends. We tend to take it out of each

[1] See, for instance: Calhoun, J. B., Population Density and Social Pathology, *Scientific American*, 1962, 2, 139-50; Morris, D., The response of animals to a restricted environment, *Symp. Zool. Soc. Lond.*, 1964, 13, 99-118; Hall, T., Proxemics. *Current Anthropology*, 1968, 9, 83-95. Hall (1968, p. 86) in his survey of the germinal studies which have contributed to his thinking, quotes Paul Errington on muskrats:
>   His studies of muskrats and their behavioural responses to the stress from crowding are most revealing. He states that *muskrats share with men* the propensity for growing savage under stress from crowding.

other as well. Lynda and Fionna have been together
for so long that sparks are beginning to fly. Peter and
Gary are the same. Even with Lisa I'm beginning to
get—you know—strained. The fights we had before
were purely fun: we just used to take things out on
each other and use each other as punch bags, you
know. But even they are beginning to get more
serious, which is bad. We're beginning to niggle each
other. You can work with a group for years and years
and years and be quite happy, but you can't live with
that group. It's almost like marriage. The whole
damn group. Each one is married to the other and I
can now see sense in divorce.

It is interesting that two others quite independently used
the image of that most stifling but supportive of institutions,
the family, to describe the group situation:

GARY You can't work with people in a situation like this
without either hating them or feeling a lot of affection
for them, and it's almost like being part of a family.
There's no privacy of any kind.

'You couldn't be neutral?'

GARY No. Impossible. You can be neutral maybe with Gavin
and Lisa because they're separated in a way but even
then I feel very close to them just because we all do
work together on the same thing and because they're
supporting us in all we're doing.

BOB It's like a family, a group like this.

It is fascinating to find that the notion of the group as:

. . . a simulation of the family constellation, (that is, through
transference members react to one another as members of their
family) with the unity and cohesion generally accepted in that
structure' (Tuckman, 1970, p. 332), constitutes a developmental stage in several 'therapy' group studies.

The stage is usually classified, as will be apparent from the quotation, as that of group cohesion and integration. What *Movable Workshop* demonstrates and what such studies fail to stress is that members, while acknowledging their bonds, may become increasingly irritated by them:

> 'I can now see sense in divorce.'

Small groups and families under unnatural strains display a tendency to scapegoat individuals.[2] The company was no exception to this classic pattern:

FIONNA This is just a job but when you think about it it's like being a student. All herded into the bus and can't do this and can't do that, and this comes right over into the evening at the hotel and in the morning.

GARY Unfortunately, though within ourselves we take it out on Peter. We get nervous and I guess it's good to have somebody to take it out on but it's a pity it's Peter who doesn't look too happy these days. It's very funny how it happens—when things suddenly get tense and one person gets picked on.

LYNDA Poor Peter tends to get most of it at the moment. You know, I like him as a person. It's just that somebody has to be the stooge for a day. It just happens to be poor Peter. In a way its because he's not as sure of himself as a dancer. But we can't all be in such close proximity all the time. It gets people at the end of their tether.

Peter himself was well aware of the cause of these tensions:

> I think that perhaps being thrown together all the time is bad. Perhaps we are beginning to see too much of each other. I get very sensitive to people's remarks

---

[2] Thus White & Lippit (1960, p. 543) report that in their experiments on setting up 'social climates' the group which was under stress and experiencing frustration from autocratic leadership manifested 'scapegoating behaviour'.

which sometimes aren't meant in an unpleasant way, but if you're tired and edgy . . . I tend to get very edgy and I know it shows, it must do. You know the people in the group, I like all of them, but there are times when you don't want to be with them and they mustn't want to be with you. At the beginning you want to be friendly and to know the others as people. I think now we've got to know each other as people and there isn't that eagerness to be with each other all the time that there was in the first place. We'd always go out together and do things together but that isn't always the case now—because we're thrown together.

Unnatural proximity brought out inevitable tensions and scapegoating but the bonds, though chaffing, were also ties that could be missed. Gary and Fionna expressed this ambivalence of feeling:

FIONNA It's funny tonight, going into a room and just shutting the door. (The company had single rooms at Fort William.) I've always shared a room with Lynda. Now you've got the opportunity to shut yourself off, and suddenly you're on your own and instead you go round seeing everyone's room to make sure they're still there.

GARY The four days I was out, ill, it was really nice. I'd just be sitting in my room all day. And it got to the point Sunday that I was going to ride in the van with Gavin. I didn't want to see anyone any more. But then, once I got back into the 'bus I just couldn't imagine not being there any more. I wanted to be back.

FIONNA It was very refreshing for me to be away, but not in any nasty sense. And it's the same on the other side. When someone's been away everyone is happy to see them again with renewed freshness.

The ecology of the dance group, whether provoking irritated frustration or warm togetherness, was extraordinary in its encapsulating integration of work, social and domestic settings. Goffman (1961, p. 5) in his study of *Asylums,* has postulated this integration as the 'central feature' of the 'total institution':

> A basic social arrangement in modern society is that the individual tends to sleep, play and work in different places, with different co-participants, under different authorities, and without an over-all rational plan. The central feature of total institutions can be described as a breakdown of the barriers ordinarily separating these three spheres of life.

His total institutions are sizable and static and have special organisational characteristics in that a small supervisory staff manage a larger group of inmates. Instances are orphanages, hospitals, prisons, boarding schools and barracks. The consequences of this bureaucratic organisation of all aspects of life are spelt out: the development of hostile stereotypes between managers and managed, and the destruction of those 'structural motivations to work' which operate outside, so that 'whether there is too much work or too little, the individual who was work-oriented on the outside tends to become demoralized by the work system of the total institution'.

Now none of these consequences applies to the dance company, yet that which Goffman postulates as a 'central feature' of total institutions holds entirely true for them. So we need to recognise that the consequences spelt out do not necessarily arise from this 'breakdown of the barriers ordinarily separating these three spheres of life' but from such variables as size of institution, types of social control utilised, the nature of the institution's interaction with the larger society around etc. And, utilising Goffman's 'central feature', we can posit a different kind of total institution, the small, mobile unit, which, without the symbolic barriers of high walls and locked doors, nevertheless 'encompasses' its members, structures their entire day's programme, and cuts them off from social intercourse with others. For the characteristic which such units share with the large, static bureaucratised institution is incompatibility:

> . . . with another crucial element of our society, the family. Family life is sometimes contrasted with solitary living, but in fact the more pertinent contrast is with batch living, for those who eat and sleep at work, with a group of fellow workers, can hardly sustain a meaningful domestic existence (Goffman, 1961, p. 11).

Functioning in a work situation where ordinary domestic and social relations were rendered impossible it is not surprising that members of *Movable Workshop* should utilise the image of 'the family' to characterise relationships within the company. For the duration of the tour, the group was the family surrogate.

Inmates of static total institutions become habituated to the institutional norms and find themselves increasingly disoriented in the world outside. A similar effect is experienced by members of mobile 'total institutions', who find themselves cut off from the normal range of social relationships. The following extracts are from a group discussion a week before the tour ended:

GARY When we're not dancing we all find there's nothing to do. I've forgotten what to do with spare time.

FIONNA It's become our sole existence. When I got locked out the other night, when Lynda was out and I hadn't a key, it suddenly occurred to me that there was no one to go to. Before I joined the group, if I'd been locked out I'd just go around to friends. But now there was no-one to go to. There was nothing to do except just sit on the stairs and wait for her to come back again.

GARY It's been really frustrating on tour. Meeting people in workshops with an ordinary calm sort of existence. They're very nice people you'd like to get to know, but you see them for an hour and never see them again. Faces here and there on tour—really nice—I thought

I'd like to get to know them. But it's impossible. The only people I can get to know are people in the group. And then we get so familiar with each other that we can't stand each other any more.

LYNDA Because we can't get away, not even for a minute, because we don't know anyone. It's either be on your own, or be with us.

FIONNA For us the present doesn't exist.

GARY It's really true. I feel like when the tour's over I'll really be living again.

PETER I get the feeling it really is like a dream.

FIONNA I went shopping this morning. I knew I had to go to rehearsal and I felt like a fraud shopper because people were lingering round counters. I was getting very cross because they wouldn't serve me and I just wished I could be an ordinary person having time to browse round. I felt like an outsider even when shopping.

LYNDA We have very little freedom.

The 'insider', on the rare occasions 'outside', feels like an 'outsider'.

All members were aware of the strains of the situation, but possibilities of escape and degrees of tolerance varied. Thus Stuart was 'maddened by all the proximity. Those interminable singing sessions in the 'bus', but could briefly retire to his own flat in Glasgow and resume, however fleetingly, existing contacts. Geoffrey, with four years of training with Festival Ballet behind him, was inured to the demands of the situation. Gavin said wonderingly of Bob, 'He's very sensitive but in a strange way he's immune. It's a contradiction.' Bob's capacity to retain his equanimity, to preserve even in proximity a psychic space around himself, enabled him to assert, 'I don't want to cut myself off from the others. I don't feel a need to cut myself off. I'm enjoying it for ten weeks.' The others did, however, feel this need, increasingly as the weeks went by.

No group can be characterised in a vacuum. As Hall (1968, p. 86) has asserted in his article on 'Proxemics':

> At the risk of stating the obvious, I wish to underscore what appears to be a growing consensus among ethologists and ecologists that the organism and its environment are so inextricably intertwined that to consider either as separate is an artefact of our own particular way of looking at things.

A work group in a factory, a discussion group in a committee room, a therapy group in a clinic, an experimental group in a laboratory, is constrained not only by the members' personalities, and by the nature of the task, but by the environmental conditions in which the group is operating. The environmental conditions of *Movable Workshop* were those of a total institution, and as such imposed considerable stress. It is an important conceptual point to recognise that 'total institutions' can exist without any confining walls. A considerable range of mobile units now manifest this 'central feature' of a 'breakdown of the barriers ordinarily separating work, social and domestic life'. This study of the ecology of *Movable Workshop* reveals the stress that such a breakdown imposes. Members of expeditions, mountaineers, explorers, crews, teams on tour, flying squads of highly specialised workers, pop groups, all are inmates of 'total institutions' and subject to similar stress. Anyone selecting personnel for such mobile units needs to take into consideration not only job expertise but personality characteristics. If brilliance and equanimity can be combined, splendid. But otherwise perhaps a less brilliant but more self-contained performer will be better suited to sustain the demands imposed. Stress can be ameliorated by the planning of time off; infrequent long breaks may be more refreshing than frequent short breaks if the short break does not allow for a genuine re-entry into the broader social context. But any member of a 'total institution' is going to experience frustration from proximity, no matter how much amelioration is provided. There should be possibilities for acknowledging this without guilt or recrimination. The wonder is not that the Beatles disbanded, but that they stayed together so long.

8

WHO AM I AND WHAT
IS DANCE?

Motivation and Task

In many cultures dance is an essential component of still
meaningful rituals. Whether the performers are amateurs or
professionals,[1] they are participating in activities which are
recognised as important to the well being of their
communities:

> Birth, circumcision, and the consecration of maidens, marriage
> and death, planting and harvest, the celebration of chieftains,
> hunting, man and feasts, the changes of the moon, and
> sickness, for all these dance is needed (Sachs, 1937, p. 11).

[1] Gorer (1945, p. 193) points out that:
> African dancers can be roughly divided into two groups: professional and
> amateur dancers. In the more primitive communities there are nearly always
> professional dancers, people who are supported by the community to do their
> dancing for them . . . The presence of professional dancers does not prevent the
> rest of the community from dancing; but on the whole they confine themselves to
> chorus work or to relatively simple round dances.

As Rust (1969, p. 11) has asserted in her study of social dance:

> In the life of primitive peoples, nothing approaches the dance in significance. It is no mere pastime, but a very serious activity. It is not a sin but a sacred act. It is not mere 'art' or 'display' divorced from the other institutions of society: on the contrary, it is the very basis of survival of the social system in that it contributes significantly to the fulfilment of all societies needs.

In Western urbanised societies dance no longer makes this fundamental contribution. Fashions in social dance are never fortuitous, and they illumine the class structure, the economic and political developments, the relationships between generations and between sexes, in our technologically advanced societies. But illumination can be shed from the periphery, and dance has become peripheral to western society's main concerns, a diversion if offered in the theatre, a minor element in the socialising processes if offered in schools. One form of diversionary dance, the ballet, has sufficient status from its aristocratic antecedents and its connections with the arts of music and design to survive as a prestigious cult. Modern dance, however, is a curiously deviant activity, participants whether performers or audience constituting a tiny minority in societies which have invested their aspirations and energies elsewhere. The fact that pioneering individuals from this minority have been able to infiltrate into the schools and colleges of the United Kingdom the teaching of a particular aspect of modern dance, that based on Laban's movement principles, can be regarded cynically as yet another instance of the arbitrary nature of the school curriculum, and of its divorce from the meaningful concerns of adult community.

Such cynicism is, however, a superficial response lacking any explanatory power. Professional educators increasingly see themselves not only as the protectors and purveyors of communal values, but as agents of change. The tension of combining both roles is, I believe, a fundamental cause of present distress amongst teachers. In a school system which reflects the current values of society in its emphasis on competition, on the cognitive, on language as the tool of manipulation, the introduction of modern educational dance is a subversive activity, a deliberate offering of alternative experiences and values. That its original proponents in the United Kingdom were white middle class gentlewomen does not render it any less deviant. But subversion needs to acquire robust sources of nourishment from society at large if it is to flourish. It is possible to view Modern Educational Dance as a somewhat precious form of self-expression encapsulated safely within the educational system. I suggest that it is more perceptive to view it as an innocent and naive early manifestation of a developing counter-culture which is revolutionary in its implications. This counter-culture recognises the body's expressive and symbolic resources, is prepared to devote scholarly attention to their meaning, is anxious to experience the body as a medium of art and is ready to utilise the body through symbolic gesture as a means of political as well as artistic statement. In *Sociology as a Skin Trade* O'Neill (1972) has illumined the ways in which the body has become 'the non-verbal rhetoric' of political dissidents'.[2] The proponents of Laban-based modern educational dance, and of Modern dance in general, by taking cognisance of this movement and by becoming self-consciously aware of this counter culture, could conceivably enable dancing to be once again linked more centrally to society's needs and concerns.

How far were the members of *Movable Workshop* aware of the historical background and the educational and social implications of their work? Why did they enter an occupation which is arduous, financially unrewarding, insecure, to the great bulk of the population irrelevant and arcane? Were they prompted by personal aspirations or devotion to group goals? Did they see themselves as individual exhibitionists motivated by applause, or as a revolutionary group offering schools and

---

[2] See: Hinde, R. A., *Non-Verbal Communication*. Cambridge: University Press, 1972; Bosmajian, H. A. (Ed) *The Rhetoric of Non-Verbal Communication*. New York: Scott, Foresman & Co, 1971; Benthall, J. & Polhemus, T. (Eds) *The Body as a Medium of Expression*. New York: Allen Lane. 1975.

society a counter-culture? Members of all work groups, no matter how apparently respectable their calling, need to justify to themselves their occupational choice. This is particularly necessary for those who enter occupations which are unorthodox and marginal. Some exploration of motivation is needed to throw light on the reasons which prompt individuals, against all rational self-interest, to take up work which is strenuous, erratic and underpaid.

I shall put on one side for the moment the motivations of Geoffrey, Gavin and Lisa since as administrative and technical staff their career choices might well have been made on a different basis from the dancers. I shall, however, include Bob, since to pursue music as a profession has some obvious analogies; in addition Bob choreographed for and danced with the company.

A study of individual backgrounds throws up some striking common factors. The dancers were of different nationalities and had parents representing a wide range of social class from barrister to taxi driver. Yet each dancer came from a family which had one or more members sympathetic to and participating in the performing arts. Thus Stuart Hopps' grandmother was an actress in the Yiddish theatre in Paris. Gary's father was an accomplished pianist and guitarist, Peter's father played saxophone in a jazz band, his mother sang in a music group and acted in amateur companies. Lynda's father, a woodwind player, was once musical director for Moss Empire theatres; he now conducts and teaches music. Fionna's mother was drama advisor for a local authority. Marita's mother was an amateur singer. Bob's elder sister teaches the guitar, his younger brother plays in a folk group. Each individual had a home background in which music making and/or acting were normal activities indulged in by one or more members of the family.

Individuals also had in common a recollection of having enjoyed dancing in childhood. Gary remembered dancing with his sister to old gramophone records: later he went to tap-dancing classes which were abandoned with embarrassment in adolescence. All three girls enjoyed dancing and were enrolled in ballet classes. Stuart, Bob and Peter mention no early formal training, but can recollect being interested in the experience of movement from an early age. All young children, of course dance:

> Most observers report that at about the age of one and a half the majority of children, without training, start some clearly recognisable rhythmical movement such as bouncing or jumping up and down in response to rhythmic music. Abandoning the word 'instinctive' as a relatively unhelpful concept when applied to human beings, one can at any rate claim that the bulk of the available evidence indicates that dancing is basically an unlearned, innate, motor/rhythmic muscular reaction to stimuli, whose function for the individual is either to express feeling or to 'work off' energy (Rust, 1969, p. 11).

In an environment crowded with breakable possessions these early innate responses are gradually inhibited. They have no market value for the technological man the child is destined to become. In a home where music or drama constitutes part of the environment, these rhythmic responses obviously have a better chance of being maintained until an age when conscious recollection becomes possible.

The other striking factor in common was the nil contribution of the school to the career choice. Only Marita in Australia and Gary in America were offered dance in the school curriculum, and its effect was negligible compared with the private tuition both experienced. Schools act as filters which channel individuals into training and job outlets and they can, of course, do this for occupations which are not represented in the curriculum. But in modern dance the training outlets other than via teacher-training are only now coming into existence and job outlets are few and precarious. The nil contribution of the school is therefore only to be expected and indeed indicates how little, in spite of pioneer efforts, modern dance is integrated into the structures of our society.

So for all the dancers apart from Marita, commitment

came in the course of alternative training for 'safe' careers. (Marita, as a classical dancer, enrolled at fifteen in a ballet school.) Stuart Hopps took a degree course in modern languages at London University: dance was a secondary activity which he followed by private study and which he developed as a career only after the completion of his degree. Peter studied at a technical college, became a laboratory technician, revived his interest in movement through work in amateur dramatics and then applied to The Place for further training. Lynda and Fionna signed at Dartington for a dance/drama/teacher training course and interest in modern dance developed as a result of the lectures offered. Gary went to the University of Maryland to study English Literature, had to take a one year physical education course, selected a dance option and found that this revived an early love of dance. Bob originally attended a college of art, took up the professional study of music at university, and developed an interest in dance after working at The Place.

Because of the dearth of training and job outlets the choice of modern dance as a career therefore occurred late and almost fortuitously. Yet behind all the divergencies lies a pattern of early delight in movement and a home background where the performing arts were participated in by some member of the family. This delight is revived at adult level by an individual teacher, a particular lecturer, a specific college course, or exposure to dance as an art form in theatre or television.

I have indicated the route by which individuals came to take up dance and have shown the irrelevance of the school and the indirect yet salient effect of the home in this process. The next stage is to probe what the experience of dancing meant to individual members, how they perceived the task of *Movable Workshop* and how they saw themselves in relation to that task.

The Group Goals

Stuart Hopps was expectedly the most articulate in expressing the company's goals. He had evolved them over a period of two years, had expressed them to his own governors and to fund-allocating bodies, had discussed them with a range of educationalists and ultimately with the dancers he recruited. Yet, as he himself explained, he had not set off with any clear cut blue print:

> I don't think I ever wanted a company as a vehicle for my ideas, that kind of company. I was never ambitious when I came back from America to form a group. I was interested in the theatre—not in performing primarily but in choreographing and directing—but I was interested in education also and in the significance of artists in society. Do they act as catalysts in society as well as being just people on the other side of the proscenium? What kind of contribution can they make outside the theatre? You could argue, 'Isn't it enough that they are making a contribution inside the theatre?' My argument is that I don't think it is enough. I think it's important for the arts to be more encompassing.

As part of a policy to make them more 'encompassing' Stuart conducted workshops and master classes in schools, colleges and universities, and from these emerged the three week Remy-Charlip-directed tour and finally *Movable Workshop*. I have summarised *Movable Workshop's* goals from discussion with Stuart and from a brief written statement he supplied:

(1) To present performances of modern dance at professional level in areas which have not had the opportunity of seeing it before.

(2) To offer workshops in which ideas developed in the performance can be explored by dancers and by members of the audience in a gymnasium or on stage.

(3) To involve audiences, and particularly young people, in dance activities which are approachable, meaningful and will engage their interest and enthusiasm.

(4) To provide a link between performer and spectator so that dance is considered not as an esoteric and remote spectacle but as a rewarding experience available to all.

(5) To provide a link between dance in education as presented

in schools and colleges and dance in the theatre.

(6) To be involved in experimentation and work of the highest professional standards alongside other artists.

Task achievement is improved if group members have an understanding of group goals. The following quotations show that members had grasped the essential; namely, the missionary purpose of bringing modern dance to the unaware by the dual strategy of performances and workshops. Lynda asserted that the aim was:

> . . . to bring a clear—simpler than usual—understanding or explanation of dance, particularly to people who don't either see or know anything of dance or who think dance is something way beyond their understanding.

FIONNA Not just presenting and exploring modern dance but using it as a means of communication. If you go into the theatre with a modern dance group you are putting a performance on the stage and there's no reason to draw the people into it. You've got to meet people half-way. That's why we are trying to do more than a performance. You've got to offer them some sort of invitation to involve themselves.

GARY It's more than just performing. It's most important we should be good performers, because people get excited if they see something really good and want to know more about it. We want to open people up to a new kind of dance. Perhaps also give some new· approaches to teaching dance in the colleges here. It all seems to stem from Laban and I have a feeling its limited and we could extend it by showing other kinds of things.

BOB To put on intriguing performance. To release the dance potential within people.

Every dancer when questioned claimed to have a moderately clear idea of what the group's goals were: this achieved by discussions with Stuart and amongst themselves. The one element in Stuart's list which was not raised by any other member was that of 'experimental work with other artists'. This was either not consciously known as an aim in spite of participation in *Columba*; was known and rejected, because of *Columba,* or was felt to be relevant to Stuart, operating as director, but not to the dancers themselves.

Individual and Group Goals

By becoming a member of a group the individual to some extent subordinates his personal aspirations. As Mayo (1949, p. 127) has asserted in a comment on Quesnay:

> In our industrial studies we, like many others, have found it to be as true today as in Quesnay's time that individual self-interest is eagerly subordinated to the group.

Yet no individual joins a group unless he believes that in some way the group will serve his personal aspirations. There must be some possibility of the group goals matching individual needs or recruitment would not take place. This reconciliation of individual satisfactions with group goals is a delicate and difficult operation. Publicly asserted group goals are usually respectable. Individual goals may smack of self-interest; their presence in one-self is admitted apologetically, in others suspected reproachfully. Public and overt goals are, of course, invariably counter-balanced by private and less disinterested motives, but these idealistic young dancers obviously had a problem in coming to terms with this complexity.

LYNDA I see the group as a very experimental thing for us. I'm experimenting in what I am doing because I don't know exactly what the group is about. It's finding out as much for myself as for anyone else what dance is about. What it means. What point it has. I suppose that sounds very much as though I'm using the group.

GARY The aims are not so clear as they used to be. I think we're meant to be introducing modern dance to

Scottish schools. I think there are other more selfish and egocentric aims.

BOB I think, strangely enough, the purposes are not all outward. Ostensibly we're here to perform, to give others the opportunity to interest themselves in dance, but obviously all the people taking part get a great stimulation from dancing. A group like this enables them to carry on what they want to do. I think to release what they have within.

'So the group serves a purpose for them as well as they serving the group's purpose.'

BOB Yes.

To assert that individuals are prompted by egocentric motives is in no sense to impugn the validity of the public, disinterested aims, yet the dancers felt an unease at admitting this complexity. It is perfectly possible, however, to combine altruism with personal ambition, concern for others with self-interest. Homans (1951, p. 95) in discussing the motivation of workers at the celebrated Hawthorne Plant, says:

> Let us be clear as to what we mean by this famous phrase (self-interest). In the first place, it may be that all motives are motives of self interest in the sense that, given the situation in which he is placed, a man always tries to do as well as he can for himself. What he does may look to outsiders as if it were hurting rather than helping him: it may look impossibly altruistic rather than selfish, and yet modern psychology teaches us that, if we knew the full situation, both the social relationships and the psychological dynamics of the person concerned, we should find all his actions to be self-enhancing.

Since Stuart was the instigator of the group, there is every reason to assume that *Movable Workshop* was intended to serve not only a perceived educational need but certain personal aspirations. As a non-classically trained choreographer operating with a classical ballet-company, the incentive to carve out separate territory where his particular strengths could be more effectively utilised would be strong. *Movable Workshop* would emerge not only in response to social and educational requirements but in response to personal anxieties and the desire for self-enhancement.

Once the group was conceptualised, members were induced to join because, in Bob's words, it enabled them 'to carry on what they want to do'. And what they wanted to do was dance.

Why did they wish to dance? What was there in the experience of dancing that induced them initially to follow an arduous training and then to join a dance company? In his study of another marginal group, dance band musicians, Howard Becker has demonstrated how reference to a distinctive life-style—more crazy, reckless and off-beat than other people's—served to reassure them as to their occupational choice. Musicians are:

> . . . just not like other people, that's all . . . Musicians live an exotic life, like in a·jungle or something. (Becker, 1963, p. 86.)

In a perceptive article on 'The Actor and His World' Taylor and Williams (1971) show how a belief in the 'magic of the theatre' and a conviction of being 'specially sensitive to this magic' enables the small town repertory actor to maintain professional faith. The group of dancers could not physically afford a reckless life-style, since their bodies were the medium of expression, nor could they invoke the 'magic of the theatre' which was conspicuously lacking in a school hall, gymnasium or community centre. How then did they explain their occupational choice?

It is interesting that they found it much more difficult to articulate what the experience of dancing meant to them as individuals than they did to state the company's public goals. Compare, for instance, Fionna's earlier statement on offering the public 'some sort of invitation to involve themselves' with her attempt to grapple with the question of her own motivation:

'You made quite a lot of financial sacrifices last year in Holland. What is it about dance that justifies this?'

FIONNA I don't know. I ask myself the same thing sometimes. I always think I won't be compelled to go on. If someone had told me before I went to Holland the sacrifices I would make, I would have said, 'Rubbish. I'm not that interested in dance.' But obviously there is a part of you which is and which compels you to do more.

'What do you think dance offers to people?'

FIONNA I think, well, getting, well, profound (Laughter) I think, well, dance is a—such a basic—I don't know. What's the word?—sort of basic. I just think that modern dance offers something that ballet doesn't and that it's very exciting, very real. You know—for people it's much more—Oh, I'm not sure what I mean, to put it into words!

It was because of this problem of 'putting it into words' that I asked the group members to write to me, after the tour had ended and they had had time to reflect, explaining the significance of dance to them. 'What are your feelings about dance? How do you know you are a dancer? What is the meaning to you of being a dancer?' The extracts which follow are thus drawn from written responses.

Marita admits to being puzzled at the compulsion to dance:

I think a lot of my initial moments are spent asking myself that very question, How do you know you are a dancer? All I do know is that even when, at the lowest ebb in my dancing life, I have tried to turn to other things I'm interested in and make a more secure career of those, I realise I can't do it.

Then comes the attempt at explanation:

It is my most successful way of expressing in a clear and genuine way what I wish to say both to others as well as to myself. When I'm on stage in front of an audience I discover a part of me that cannot escape by any other means.

Fionna writes:

I find it much easier to answer this now, having worked for the past two weeks in an office. I am beginning to realise not only that I enjoy dancing but that in order to endure a day working at something that I do not get anything from, I need to know that at the end of the day I will be able to go and take a dance class. Dance gives me satisfaction as a means of expressing myself. Perhaps I would say that I am a dancer not only technically but spiritually in that I begin to feel a strong dedication to the art and will sacrifice time and financial benefit to pursue it further.

These statements go beyond a reiteration of a somewhat mysterious dedication and imply that the act of dancing is part of a process of self discovery, self realisation and self expression.

Lynda asserts:

It was a fulfilment. I enjoyed every dancing and teaching moment, and the learning times too. I miss it physically. I have terrific stores of energy which don't get used up when I'm not dancing. Physical energy, not mental, so that I feel I have to run fast round the fields sometimes to use it up. It's exhilarating; mentally stimulating and physically stimulating in that the use of energy creates more energy. It's a form of communication. It fulfils every requirement that an energetic person can have.

Yet Lynda, whose talents and versatility made an impact in every workshop and performance, is anxious to cut through any mystique. With that bracing, clear sighted realism that was a great source of her strength in the group, she admits:

> Yet it can't have been enough for me, because I was wanting to do other things too. There are people who are dedicated to one aspect of life—dancing, furniture-making, teaching. I was never dedicated to dancing, only to doing as well as I could something I enjoyed. I've never thought of myself as a dancer. Just a person who enjoyed dancing and happened to be asked to join a dance company. Dancers are those ethereal people you see on stage who can do such wonderful things with such grace and fire. No, I don't think of myself as a dancer. And dance is just something I enjoy doing. I think it would be hard to find a dancer who actually *needed* to dance. I think the majority of dancers are people who have found they can dance; they enjoy it and since it's possible to earn a living at it, that's what they do. No, that's not true, because all dancers struggle to get better and better, and I can't explain that or understand it.

So the personal experience of dance is conveyed with a deliberate down-to-earth realism which nevertheless breaks down as Lynda admits to a sense of wonder at the dancer's inexplicable struggle for perfection. What can be explained, however, is the delighted use of physical energy, the exhilarating sense of fulfilment in this utilisation of the body as a means of communication.

Peter writes:

> Dance has always been important to me since I was very young. It has always seemed to say a lot to me, I don't really know why.
> The meaning of being a dancer to me? Expression through physical power. The control of one's body in a

meaningful and beautiful way. And the fulfilment of a
life long ambition. The theatre has always attracted
me and dancing is just an extension of this attraction.

How do I know that I am a dancer? That's a
question I am still asking myself. The fact is that I'm
not sure I am a dancer except perhaps in my mind
where it has always been. It's sad, but the standard
that I have fixed for myself as a dancer is too perfect
for me to attain. Ask me this question again in five
years.

Peter's modest refusal to admit to being a dancer is akin to
the discrepancy expressed by Lynda between the ideal
creature doing 'wonderful things with such grace and fire' and
the earth bound, limited human:

> Between the idea
> And the reality
> Between the motion
> And the act
> Falls the Shadow.

Yet his statement shows that he finds dance both a gratifying
mode of expression and a source of aesthetic satisfaction, and
thus the media through which he hopes to realise his ambition
to perform in the theatre.

Gary starts his credo with a characteristically wry deflation:

> If I were to say that dance is my life it would sound
> very corny. I could probably live without dancing.

He then adds:

> But I don't want to. I never feel so alive or so aware of
> myself as when I'm dancing. There are rare mystical
> moments on stage when one is moving perfectly.
> There is no block between mind and body. Everything
> flows freely, and whatever one does will be 'right'.
> There is no past or future, just an eternal present, an

eternal presence that uses you as an instrument through which it can make itself known to the audience. Art is a search for the truth and for a way to communicate that truth to others. A dancer works hard to perfect his technique so that when the time comes it will not be him dancing, but, if you will allow me, God dancing. A dancer is an 'acrobat of God', always reaching, struggling, growing, and what he learns of life and of truth is what he conveys on the stage. That is why it is so important to dance accurately, to let God within you, God within the choreography, come through, not just a sordid collection of egos.

I think we would all be dancers if only we had the awareness of what we are doing. Walking down the street is dancing. Brushing your teeth is dancing. It is all dancing if one is only aware of it. That awareness is what makes a dancer. What is seen on stage is only heightened reality, concentrate of reality. One of the aims of dance is to show how beautiful life can be, how we can take the same beauty we see on stage into our lives.

To Gary dance is a form of heightened perception when mind and body are perfectly attuned, and such moments can be experienced not only in the dance artefact but in all physical activities.

To Bob, one of the gratifications of both music making and dancing is to experience an action and then to register through the perceptions the feedback from that action:

One of the most pleasurable things for me personally is to act then to feel the ripples caused by the action through the perceptions, whether those ripples have come only a short simple route or a complex one. For example, I might be sitting alone at the piano and strike a chord which surprises and excites me. The movement of my hands has passed through the piano

action to the string, to the air, to my ear, and back to
me. A more complex route might be exemplified by
reading a review of the *Workshop* where one's actions
pass through another person, the reviewer, the hands
of the type setter, and the newspaper before reaching
the source again.

In dancing I find again both simple and complex
loops; the simple—making a movement and feeling
the agreeable sensations in the muscles and the
circulation of the blood and the lightness of
mood—the more complex, hearty laughter or
exclamations or other responses coming from an
audience.

Another thing I can identify as bringing pleasure to
me is organisation: the sudden noticing of a way a
thing is constructed, of a relationship it may have with
something seemingly far removed, i.e. analysis and
synthesis. Both music and dance are highly organised
though not necessarily regular and foursquare. Often
the organisation is delicate and elusive.

What emerges from these personal statements, these
subjective accounts of the meaning of being a dancer? Very
clearly, an expression of delight in physical energy, a
savouring of the sensations of moving effectively. These
dancers are humans who have not been alienated from the
body but who relish the sensations of muscular tone, strength
and speed, weight and lightness. They enjoy the perceptual
feedback from their actions and exemplify what Murray
(1964, p. 79) in his survey of theories of motivation has
termed 'intrinsically motivated behaviour', that is, 'the
pleasurable use of one's perceptual apparatus and one's
muscular apparatus'. Additionally, for the dancers the body
is not only a cource of sensations but is perceived as having
symbolic resources. The expressive qualities of the human
form, exploited in dance, are a source of gratification in that
the dancer has in the body a powerful means of communication. Moreover, dancing involves the experiencing

of a wide physical and emotional range, contrasting capacities for strength and delicacy, aggression and tenderness, awe and derision etc and is therefore felt as a source of self-discovery. 'Self discovery' and 'self expression' are terms frequently employed by the individual members in their attempts to explain the meaning of dance to them.

Aesthetic pleasure is derived from a realisation of the body's power, elegance, grotesqueness etc, and from its utilisation in relation to space, to other bodies, to the environment. This aesthetic pleasure is at its most intense during participation in a dance artefact but can be experienced, as Gary claims, in unchoreographed movement activities.

Curl (1974, p. 36) in a convincing application to physical skills of Professor Hepburn's arguments on the aesthetic aspects of nature, argues that aesthetic response need not be distanced, detached and reflective, but can be involved, immediate and simultaneous:

> To transpose Professor Hepburn again, 'the skilful performer is both performer and spectator, ingredient in his skilful activity, aware of the sensations of being thus ingredient, directing his skilfulness and letting his skilfulness feed back and enrich his awareness of himself in that skilfulness. This is not to suggest that his skilful attention is being reduced by irrelevant preoccupations, but merely to say that his aesthetic perceptions are ingredient to, and simultaneous with his performance—and appreciated as such.

Heightened responsiveness to sensations, the feeling of mind and body in harmony, appreciation of the aesthetic may be expressed by Gary in terms of mystical awareness or by Bob in cognitive terms:

> Another thing I can identify as bringing pleasure to me is organisation: the sudden noticing of a way a thing is constructed, of a relationship it may have with something seemingly far removed.

How can these varied personal statements, with their highly individual forms of expression, be related to explicit theories of motivation? I have already argued (p. 139) that one element indicated by them falls readily into 'intrinsically motivated behaviour'. But the theory of motivation which has most explanatory power in relation to the complex range of gratifications cited by the dancers is, I suggest, that of Maslow. Maslow (1954, p. 99) freely admits the exploratory nature of his research and the tentative quality of his theorizing:

> This kind of research is in principle so difficult—involving as it does a kind of lifting oneself by one's axiological bootstraps—that if we were to wait for conventionally reliable data, we should have to wait for ever.

But the conclusions he draws from his investigations are penetrating, rich in their implications, and the only ones adequate to encompass the accounts of their experience given by the dancers. Maslow admits the validity of the concept of 'basic needs' which 'had been assumed to be the only motivations for human beings' but he adds to these, in a hierarchical structure, the 'meta need' for self actualisation:

> First come the physiological motives, like hunger.
> Then safety motives, like fear.
> Then love motives.
> Then esteem motives.
> Finally 'self actualisation'

The physiological motives appear early, the esteem ones later, and self actualisation if it appears at all only operates when the lower motives have been satisfied:

> Growth is seen then not only as progressive gratification of basic needs to the point where they 'disappear', but also in the form of specific growth motivations over and above these basic needs, e.g. talents, capacities, creative tendencies, constitutional potentialities. We are thereby helped also to realize that basic needs and self-actualization do not contradict each other any more than do childhood and maturity. One passes into the other and is a necessary pre-requisite for it (Maslow, 1962, p. 24).

Self actualisation is a concept drawn from Goldstein, but it has been made more specific by Maslow and signifies the striving to actualise what one is potentially, the desire to realise one's latent possibilities, the creative urge towards self-fulfilment.

Phrases used by the dancers relate significantly to this concept:

'to release what they have within'

'I believe movement was latent within me' (Bob)

'to discover a part of me that cannot escape by any other means' (Marita)

'a fulfilment' (Lynda)

'I'm not sure I am a dancer, except in my mind where it has always been' (Peter)

'I am a dancer not only technically but spiritually' (Fionna)

'To let God within you, God within the choreography, come through' (Gary)

By means of the dance, individuals in *Movable Workshop* strove to realise their potential, enact their latent aspirations, accomplish in some measure this self actualisation. Self actualising persons achieve, in Maslow's terms, certain peak experiences. A 'peak experience' is:

> . . . an episode, or a spurt in which the powers of the person come together in a particularly efficient and intensely enjoyable way, and in which he is more integrated and less split, more open for experience, more idiosyncratic, more perfectly expressive or spontaneous, or fully functioning, more creative, more humorous, more egotranscending, more independent of his lower needs, etc. He becomes in these episodes more truly himself, more perfectly actualising his potentialities, closer to the core of his Being (Maslow, 1962, p. 91).

It is their awareness of these peak experiences that individuals struggled to express to me, and the possibility of encountering such experiences provided Stuart and the dancers with their motivation for dancing, and compensated for the discomfort and insecurity inherent in their career choice.

Peak experiences, though not limited to performances, are more likely to arise in performances. But the strategies of *Movable Workshop* were, as we have seen, dual: members had to undertake not only a performing role but a teaching role. Lynda was equally happy in both:

> Workshops excite me. The things that children and adults who have never done any sort of moving before—the amazing ideas they come out with which a trained dancer would never think of. It's exciting. I don't prefer either performing or the workshop. I enjoy both.

The rest of the dancers, though selected on the basis of the dual requirement, nevertheless preferred performing:

> GARY   I really like performing most of all, because it's so exciting. It's good for the ego and there's something very satisfying about presenting yourself to an audience. We've chosen not just to be dancers but to be people other people can relate to, so that when we're in the workshops people will like us and we'll be able to talk to children. I think that's the most important thing we have. But personally I'd rather work the other way, as a performer.

> PETER   I must say I feel a bit out on a limb in the workshops because I haven't done any teaching before.

> MARITA   It's marvellous the effect it has on children. I really think, though, we should be in school for two days. There's no build up and this can be a bit frustrating. Workshops to me are quite a strain. I've loved children all my life, but not in those circumstances.

Membership of the group meant a commitment to the teaching task which was fully accepted:

GARY I think what we're doing is very good. It's very valuable. Someone has to be doing this sort of work.

But as the tour continued increasingly the dancers yearned for a pure performing role. A dual task will always impose some tensions in that one aspect of the work will come to be preferred over the other. Though the dancers identified with the group goals, it was apparent that certain individual aspirations as performers had to be held in check. The group was at one and the same time the means of satisfying, and frustrating, individual needs.

I have discussed motivation in terms of individual needs, of the struggle for self actualisation. I found no trace in discussion of commitment to the group as an instrument of revolutionary change. The dancers were a-political: they saw themselves not as outsiders coming in to disrupt, but as the allies of those teachers who were working from within the system to develop a more sensitive, more affective, more creative approach to learning. So although a genuine missionary zeal irradiated their work, there was no revolutionary fervour. The zeal was to make available to individuals, through dance, those possibilities for self actualisation that they had glimpsed for themselves. Yet in sharing their infectious delight in movement, in demonstrating the potent symbolism of the body and in joyously devising aesthetic experiences through the human form, they were quiet revolutionaries, inexplicit agents of a counter culture. This counter culture has the potential to redress the balance for the verbal, cognitive, technological human alienated from his own sensations and from his bodily potential.

What of the motivations of the non-dancing members of the group? How far did the group task match their individual needs? Lisa's own statements show that, as with the dancers, she was from an early age drawn to the performing arts.

I always adored concerts, music—used to play records
the whole time. When I was seven I managed to go to
elocution classes but I really wanted to go to ballet
and singing. I tend to live in a bit of a fantasy. When I
was older I was in an amateur company—a very good
one and we did 'The Merry Widow' for a week. The
highlight for me was at the end when the audience
applauded. The curtain calls, the coming forward—I
could really feel my eyes filling. My father said, 'This
is just a dream. Why can't you be sensible?' But then
I'd think, 'Why be sensible?'

Lisa's dream was to perform in some capacity and she was
engagingly frank in admitting to being 'stage-struck'. Yet for
all her claims 'to live in a bit of a fantasy' Lisa had an
energetic capacity for coping with reality: she accepted the job
as wardrobe mistress and her dreams ended in sewing,
laundering and pressing. She saw her task in the group not as
an end in itself, but as a means to an end, yet the discrepancy
between her task and her private dream was acknowledged
with humour and the job was tackled with enthusiasm. Lisa
will either realise her ambition or will adjust her dreams to the
feasible. She demonstrates that it is perfectly possible to carry
out the group task effectively and with commitment, even if
there is a discrepancy between that and personal needs. The
proviso is that the group task should be seen as a means to an
end, a stage towards the fulfilment of individual aspirations.

Gavin was no actor/dancer manqué. His interests were
firmly in the technical processes, the illusion, communication
through hardware. The stage manager's task with a small
touring group made many of the wrong demands. There was a
great deal of packing, unpacking, driving, sheer physical
labour. Equipment was limited and opportunities for
spectacular effects nil. Gavin's personal interest was in film
making and television and he would have enjoyed the
opportunity for more creative work than the tour allowed him.
So in that way the group's task imposed its frustrations:

Physically it's hell. At the end of the day I'm really done in. But technically, intellectually, creatively it's undemanding for me; sometimes I feel I'm just a glorified van driver.

But *Movable Workshop* provided professional experience on the technical side, which is what Gavin wanted from it. Also, after having worked as a petrol pump attendant for a brief period after leaving college, Gavin saw the group task as in itself worthy of respect. He had the satisfaction of feeling he was essential to that task:

> The dancers are absolutely shagged out at the end of the day and I couldn't ask any of them to help me strip down the stuff. My job is to reassure them that everything is going O.K. with the technical side. Tell them, 'I'll do such and such for you.' I agree with the *Workshop* and the idea is very, very good. I think we've done some good in Scotland. I think the surface has been scratched which is important. I hope *Workshop* rides again—it's an experience worth doing. There are certain rewards, even though it's a very strange pastime.

Geoffrey Macnab's interest in the theatre focused on the technical side and he completed a Diploma in Technical Theatre at the Royal Academy of Dramatic Arts. His first job was as assistant stage manager with Festival Ballet, and his interest in administration only developed when he acted as personal assistant to Beryl Grey and became involved in planning. A year's course in administration with the Arts Council confirmed him in this career choice and he joined Scottish Ballet as assistant administrator. Since he collaborated at every stage with Stuart Hopps in the emergence of *Movable Workshop,* it can be assumed, as with Stuart, that the group provided a means of fulfilling not only altruistic educational intentions but personal aspirations. Geoffrey's enjoyment of the theatre as an environment was apparent from the ease with which he could take on a variety of roles, acting in times of crisis as on-stage commentator and leader in a workshop group. His decision to focus on administration arose not only from a hardheaded realisation that, in spite of this enjoyment, his talents were technical rather than performing, but from a strong conviction of the importance of effective administration in the artistic endeavour. Efficient administration was necessary to get a group-venture off the ground and to sustain it once launched. The public relations side of the enterprise, the encounters with individuals, brought a human element into the administrative task which Geoffrey, with his easy appreciation of the quirks of personality, enjoyed. The meshing of details, the time tables, the routes, the hotel bookings, the smooth interlocking of all these were a source of gratification; authority and power derived from meticulous planning. It is significant that at the end of the tour Geoffrey said, 'I felt worst when I said goodbye to the old 'bus. It had carried us around all those weeks and never let us down.' The vehicle for *Movable Workshop* was efficient administration and that, too had never let them down:

> From my point of view, of course, the important thing to me was that all the arrangements had been successful. I'd five minutes of self congratulation. The administration had gone smoothly, as planned.

Dancers know that their career is precarious and short: their motivation as I have suggested, must be prompted by a desire for self actualisation. Administration is more long term and secure, a less risky and more rational choice. Geoffrey's comments on his own career were invariably realistic and down to earth. For his peak experiences it is possible that his possession of a private pilot's licence allowed for the fusion of meticulous planning, technical skill, with soaring 'self actualisation'!

9

WHO DECIDES?

Interpretations of Power

and Authority

Leadership is not an attribute of personality but a social role within a group.[1] Although every group situation involves

[1] See, for example, Gibb, C. A., The principles and traits of leadership. In C. A. Gibb (Ed) *Leadership*. Harmondsworth: Penguin, 1969, p. 205:

The search for leaders has often been directed towards finding those persons who have this trait well developed. The truth would seem, however, to be quite different. In fact, viewed in relation to the individual, leadership is not an attribute of the personality but a quality of his role within a particular and specified social system.

Also Bavelas, A., Leadership: man and function. In C. A. Gibb (Ed) *Leadership*, Harmondsworth: Penguin, 1969, pp. 17-24:

Traits are, after all, statements about personal characteristics. The objection to this is that the degree to which an individual exhibits leadership depends not only on *his characteristics*, but also, on the *characteristics of the situation* in which he finds himself.

To put it another way, when specific institutional patterns are different from organization to organization, one cannot say what personal traits will lead to acknowledged leadership. Instead, one must try to define the leadership functions that must be performed in those situations and regard as leadership those acts which perform them . . .

In these terms, we come close to the notion of leadership, not as a personal quality, but as an *organizational function*.

decision-taking, these decisions can be so habitual or trivial that no leadership is called for. If a group has conscious purposes to which a number of members accede, however, then every decision in relation to those purposes constitutes leader-like behaviour, irrespective of who decides. If, in addition to conscious purposes, members manifest differentiation of task roles, then the group constitutes an organisation, no matter how miniature. Power in organisations has been classified by Etzione (1964), as *coercive,* that is, based on the application of physical means, *utilitarian,* based on material rewards, or *normative,* based on symbols of prestige, esteem, love and acceptance. Though a single form of control may predominate, most organisations employ more than one. The type of control utilised affects the type of compliance. Thus coercive power is usually more alienating, remunerative induces a more calculative involvement, and normative a more committed. Control in *Movable Workshop* was both utilitarian and normative, the rules and monetary rewards being formalised in members' contracts, and socialisation being enhanced by the 'high scope' of the organisation. Organisational scope is determined by the number of activities carried out jointly by participants in a particular organisation, maximum scope being achieved by total institutions such as convents:

> High scope enhances normative control because it separates the participants from social groups other than the organisation and tends to increase their involvement in it (Etzione, 1964, p. 72).

The dancers' strong commitment to the group can be interpreted, then, as a response to a particular form of control within an organisation that embraces a wide range of their activities.

The responsibility for decision-taking was formally invested in Stuart Hopps, as Associate Director of the Ballet Company, and in Geoffrey Macnab, as Associate Administrator. Decisions relating to the artistic side of the enterprise, that is, decisions as to the choreography of dances,

content of workshops, deployment of dancers were Stuart
Hopps' prerogative. Decisions as to expenditure, specific
bookings, practical arrangements in schools and colleges,
travel schedules, were Geoffrey Macnab's. In an organisation combining authority based on knowledge (termed
'professional' authority by Etzione) and administrative
authority, clashes can easily occur. Administrators can be
perceived as insensitive to the creative aspects of the work,
unaware of artistic needs, concerned primarily with balance
sheets: artistic directors as impervious to practicalities,
demanding the impossible and impatient of financial
constraints. Etzione (1964, p. 84) states that organisations
most frequently resolve this dilemma by appointing the
professionally oriented administrator:

> The advantages of specialised administrators over lay
> administrators are obvious. They are trained for their particular
> role and have considerable understanding of the organisation in
> which they are about to function before they enter it. They are
> sensitised to the special tensions of working with professionals
> and they share some of their professional values.

Geoffrey Macnab, with his personal interest in dance, his
experience in theatre technology and his Arts Council training is clearly classifiable as a 'professionally oriented'
administrator and his effective working relationship with
Stuart Hopps is explicable on this basis. Conditions on tour
could be intensely trying, artistic standards could fluctuate,
yet each could respect the criteria underlying the other's
decisions. 'Who decides?' was clearcut on the basis of role
definition, and what was decided found joint acceptance on
the basis of shared goals and values.

So much for a conventional, systems-type analysis of
Movable Workshop as an organisation. Such an analysis is
elegant but limited. Implicit within it is a view of the
organisation as an impersonal force with leanings towards
congruence and efficiency. Inadequate for large organisations, such a view is particularly inappropriate for
one so small that it retains the characteristics of a primary

group. If the social world is a subjectively meaningful construct, then organisations as part of that social world are subjectively meaningful constructs and can only be understood in terms of the meanings which individuals attach to them. As Silverman (1972, pp. 221-2) has argued in his advocacy of an 'Action' approach to organisational theory:

> Beginning from the subjectively meaningful nature of social life, it has been argued that explorations of social action arise from the definitions of the situation and the purposes of the actors. Seen in this light, social relations within organisations arise out of the interaction of the participants and may exhibit varying levels of consensus or conflict and of co-operation and coercion, according to the nature of the expectations and ends of the actors.

Then carrying this emphasis on subjective meaning into the specific area of 'styles of supervision' (which can be interpreted to include styles of decision-taking) Silverman (1972, p. 224) points out that:

> 'Authoritarian' supervision . . . might be perceived by those who employ it or experience it in a different way than by the observer: for instance the supervisor might see it as the only means of enforcing his wishes on a recalcitrant or uninterested work group, while the workers might interpret it as an illegitimate attempt to limit their just rights. Or, in a society where traditional authority was predominant, both parties might regard such behaviour as a legitimate exercise of authority and would not think of questioning it. It would merely be the customary act of superiors and would not be interpreted as a strategy to obtain personal ends. On the other hand, 'democratic' supervision might not be a meaningful concept in such a society, while in industrial societies it might, in different contexts, be defined as either a tactic to be distrusted or a normal due of subordinates.
>
> The point here is that where the meaning (and hence possibly the legitimacy) of an action differes, to impose one definition on it, without reference to the actors' views of what is going on, can seriously distort analysis.

The key questions to ask, therefore, are not only 'Who decides?' and 'What does he decide?' but 'With what meanings does he invest his decision-taking?' and 'With what meanings is his decision-taking invested by other group members?' It is inappropriate and misleading to classify styles of leadership as 'authoritarian', 'democratic' or '*laisez-faire*' on the classic Lewin, Lippit and White (1939) model unless they are experienced as such by decision takers and their followers. What is needed to illumine decision-taking processes is the collection and analysis of participants' views.

In the early stages of *Movable Workshop* when the company were carrying out preliminary rehearsals in Glasgow there was very considerable sharing of decision-taking and frequent consultation between Stuart and the dancers. Opinions were sought as to which potential members would prove compatible to the existing group. Lynda accepted some responsibility for the choice of Larry in preference to David:

> I think it happened this way partly because of me. I think my having talked to Stuart influenced him a bit.

Suggestions were put forward by individual dancers, workshop ideas tossed around, specific choreographies evolved. Each member contributed and the contributions were evaluated not only by Stuart but by the company's reactions of approval or rejection. Stuart himself described the style of leadership necessary to the enterprise as 'strong but flexible' combining 'drive' with 'democracy':

> One of the things I wasn't sure about,—I'm still not sure—is whether I can run a group. Simply if one has the personality and is able to be strong enough and at the same time flexible enough so that the group is fairly democratic but at the same time isn't—there must be a clear drive behind it.

He adds that he wants members:

to be catalysts and to share expertise in as wide a way
as possible without dissipating it. Simply, I want them
to feel they can expand in any way they want to go.

Members enjoyed the sense of being involved in the problem-
solving processes. Fionna comments that she feels at ease
working with Stuart because:

> . . . of understanding—as far as Stuart does—what
> we hope to achieve. It's an experiment so you can't
> assess the end as yet. You can only speculate.

'You have had sessions of speculation, have you?'

Yes, very much so.

Gary approves of a working style which is challenging but
unaggressive:

> I really like working with Stuart. He has a very
> different approach to things than anyone I've worked
> with before. He keeps demanding things from me
> technically and I say 'Stuart, I can't do it.' I can do it,
> of course, and I just have to work harder. He'll never
> accept that if I say I can't do it I can't. He'll just nod
> or something and that's it. I have to do it. So he really
> makes me work and extend myself.

In order to clarify a point I asked Lynda directly how she
would characterise the way the group was being run.

LYNDA I don't think I could.

> 'Could you imagine a group being run differently and
> if so could you describe that? What would be
> different?'

LYNDA Oh. I see.

'You know, if you can't specify what it is can you specify what it isn't?'

LYNDA Yes. Well, that one could run a group that was very much dominated by its director and his ideas were always used. That he was there all the time disciplining the group. Thoroughly in charge. Completely in charge. And Stuart isn't. Partly because he has so many things to do and partly because he doesn't want to impose all his own ideas—he wants ideas from us.

'Do you express your ideas in discussion.'

LYNDA In all ways, in terms both of ideas and particular dances. Fionna is choreographing something and so is Larry and Gary's going to. Also we teach dances to each other. We help to discipline each other if you like. It's nice not to have it only Stuart.

These views coalesce into a meaningful representation of a leadership style which is consultative, demanding but low-profiled, generous in the provision of opportunities. If we apply Fiedler's (1969) contingency model of leadership we perceive a niceness of fit with one of the 'ideal types'. Fiedler's (1969, p. 236) model was innovatory in that it coped with some of the complexities of the leader-follower situation by relating three variables, (1) leader-member relations (2) task structure and (3) power of leader's position, and by positing that effective leadership was contingent on the appropriateness of these elements:

The permissive, non-directive, human-relations oriented approach is most appropriate in two types of situation. In one the leader deals with a group which is engaged in a highly unstructured task, such as one requiring problem-solving, decision-making or creativity. Here, the liked leader must be non-threatening, permissive, and group-centred, since he must depend upon the contributions of the members . . . The second type of situation is one in which the not-too-well accepted leader has a structured job.

The first situation and the correspondingly appropriate style of leadership clearly matches the early experience of members of *Movable Workshop* as recounted by them.

Columba produced a drastic change. With the existence of a script—even a script being re-worked—and a tight time schedule the period of leisurely exploration ended. The close contact with the dancers was no longer feasible and consultations were now being held with participants outside the original group. To Stuart the demands of the task were professionally over-riding. He expected that this would be recognised, and that those habits of opinion-sounding and questioning would be perceived as no longer relevant under the compelling necessity to be ready for the opening night. To the dancers, however, the social world of the *Columba* experience was confused and muddled: their views of reality fragmented and lacked cohesion. Mutual misunderstanding was strong just because earlier rapport had been well established. A breakdown of understanding accompanied the breakdown of familiar problem-solving procedures.

At this stage, after *Columba* had been successfully though painfully launched, and rehearsals for the tour re-started, Stuart exerted managerial responsibility. He made decisions on certain items in the repertoire and appointed two dancers, Peter and Marita. Peter was known to the group and linked with the earlier days of consultation. Marita was unknown. Gary, Fionna and Lynda commented to me on the situation:

GARY It's as if he has gone back on what he said about the kind of group he wanted. He's telling us. He doesn't really want our ideas.

FIONNA This new girl he's brought—he hasn't told us anything about her or discussed with us whether she'll be all right.

LYNDA Gary and I know one or two who might do but he's just brought this girl along.

This reversal of leadership pattern could be explained on the Fiedler model as an appropriate reaction to a new work situation. It was necessary to take charge if the group were not to fall apart, and Marita had certain strengths which the company needed at that point. But the reason for unilateral action went deeper. In a face-to-face group there can be no cushioning of reactions. Any leader, unless insensitive, is vulnerable to the responses of those being reluctantly led. This powerful element of reciprocal inter-action will affect the leadership style:

STUART The only thing now is to tell them what to do. I'm carrying the can for this next tour. It's my responsibility to see that items are of a certain standard. I can't allow half-finished work to be performed. I admit I'm disappointed in them so the only thing to do is let them know from now on that they're my decisions.

We have recognised that leadership-styles are contingent on the nature of the task and the relationship between leader and members. In a dynamic, on-going situation both elements can change. It is important to stress that just as leader behaviours' affect members, so members' responses can powerfully affect leader attitudes and the style of subsequent decisions. Leaders are not immune nor members impassive. Stuart's actions were to him a legitimate response to the urgent demands of a situation and to members' hurtful failure to realise the problems of his position. Members interpreted his actions as a confirmation of the gulf which had developed and a denial of the consultative procedures of the early days.

I have earlier described the stage that followed *Columba* as one of consciously renewed cohesion in which the group re-established the close working relationship which had been strained by the three-week production. But the early dependence was over and the dancers realised that they had gained in detachment and professional maturity. Gary's comment was:

I think we've all become much stronger. Now we've got on to a good working basis. Not so much emotional garbage gumming up the works.

It is interesting that in mid-tour, when Stuart was called to London because of his father's sudden illness, the group was able to take his absence in its stride. An important week-end engagement at Aberdeen lay ahead, with performances plus workshops with children and with groups of teachers. I was present when Gary, who had conducted a workshop there with Stuart the previous summer, gave a preview to the others of what lay ahead:

> We'll split into groups but it won't be like any other workshops. These teachers will know just what they want. They are very experienced, very creative, full of ideas.

In Stuart's sudden absence he had taken on a leadership role in briefing the company and reassuring them as to what lay ahead.

During the tour of the schools, all members had a certain autonomy. Lisa and Gavin were responsible for their specific areas, Bob and the dancers had some scope for decision-taking in workshops and even in the performance during improvised sections. But inevitably a great many events were structured in advance and independence of action strictly limited. Stuart and Geoffrey between them decided on such immediate issues as the timing of events, the nature of the programme, the sequence of items and the allocation of space. Because both were present each day, leadership was now obviously dual. Peter had earlier commented that a group always moans about whoever is in charge:

> I think because you need something to moan about. Not in a malicious kind of way but to let off nervous energy. I think that's fairly general. Someone has to

be in charge and must expect a certain amount of moaning.

Now there was a second target:

GARY Geoffrey's taken on the role of the bad guy. Telling us to do this and to do that! So Stuart can be out of that. He can even take our side and say, 'Oh, let's get there later in the morning, say eight o'clock'.

It is tempting to read into this dual situation a manifestation of the phenomena of 'task leader' and 'expressive leader'. Bales (1955) and his co-workers have demonstrated in their studies of problem-solving groups that almost invariably one individual emerges who assumes responsibility for the completion of the task, and another who attends to the emotional needs of the group. This concept of specialisation into instrumental and expressive roles has admittedly proved useful in analysing the dynamics of work groups and the structure of organisations. But it must be remembered that the groups which Bales studied were laboratory groups with contrived tasks. Verba (1961) has pointed out that in such groups the exercise of leadership is seen as arbitrary and a personal challenge. Carter *et al* (1960) have demonstrated that the individual who takes control in a short-term leaderless group is usually the most aggressive person present. It follows that his action is likely to be resented and an expressive leader will emerge to cope with the emotional reactions. But in long-term natural groups specialisation is by no means inevitable and one person may combine both instrumental and expressive roles. *Movable Workshop* members were committed to the task of the group. There were differences of opinion as to how that task could best be tackled, differences of taste and aesthetic judgement to be resolved. But the task itself was a means of self actualisation, and therefore effective task-leadership was also effective expressive leadership and could be combined in the one person. In the *Columba* episode the task was to some extent

resisted by certain members and Stuart, while maintaining
task leadership, lost the expressive. This was an episode, and
there was no essential reason on the rest of the tour for
dichotomy. There would thus be a spurious neatness in
casting Stuart in the specialist role of expressive leader during
the tour, Geoffrey as instrumental. Both assumed both roles
in relation to certain features; or rather, their leadership when
successful could embrace both elements. As Fionna said:

> We did miss Geoffrey in the two days he was off. I
> mean, its nice to have someone to take care of the
> administration and to be around when you're meeting
> people.

And Lynda commented:

> I think Geoffrey has to be very sharp sometimes to
> keep his leadership because he's very friendly with us.
> He's one of us, one of the gang; then he's got to do
> something to assert himself.

To confirm the complexities of the situation and to
underline the importance of members' interpretations of
events I shall look at one further episode. Since Stuart's
background was in modern dance and education, and
Geoffrey's in work with a ballet company and administration,
both had acquired somewhat differing concepts of the nature
of authority. Geoffrey obliquely revealed this when he
explained what he felt were the contrasts between 'classical'
and 'modern' dancers—we were watching a training session at
the time:

> You can't compare this group with a classical
> company. It's so different. The classical dancers
> might think the exercises look easy, but if they tried
> them these dancers would have the edge on them. But
> the classical are more professional. They work all the
> time on their performance. They'll practice endlessly
> but *then they'll do what you tell them.* (My italics.)

> These are always trying to find themselves. The
> classical are for the performance: these, what will the
> dance do for me?

This questioning, self-searching attitude carried over from the
dance into the total situation. At Golspie a meeting was
organised in the evening so that certain emergent problems
could be resolved. The immediate issue arose from a decision
Stuart had taken earlier that day. At Inverness two workshops
were held, each in a separate school. One involved teachers,
the other, children. Stuart had retained Gary, Lynda and Bob
for the teachers and had sent Fionna, Marita, Peter and
Gavin to the other. The latter felt that in this workshop
situation they were a weak second team relegated to the less
important task. The meeting was to give them opportunity to
express their feelings and to suggest different ways of dividing
in future. The other issue was to deal with the reorganisation
of the training classes, which had been temporarily
abandoned. In the meeting the atmosphere was frank but
constructive. Every person, including the non-dancers,
offered their comments. Though complaints were expressed
with restraint, they were expressed. Not all undercurrents
were admitted, but the reticences seemed designed to be non-
hurtful rather than evasive. Stuart and all the members
responded to each other with consideration and without
defensiveness. The outcomes were positive in that arrangements for reorganising the training classes were
agreed upon. To me, as observer, the session seemed an
instance of 'democracy' at work. To Geoffrey it carried a
different meaning. He suddenly intervened with a sharp
statement, the gist of which was that the group were being
well paid and well-treated and oughtn't to forget it. If they
were in the main company they would do just as they were
told, without any of this argument. The reaction of the group
was so shocked that it was apparent that the dancers and
Stuart had shared my interpretation of what was going on.
This episode provides a striking instance of the subjective
nature of the social world and reinforces Silverman's (1972)
warning:

Where the meaning (and hence possibly the legitimacy) of an action differs, to impose one definition on it, without reference to the actors' views of what is going on, can seriously distort analysis.

What to myself and to the rest of the group was a democratic way of airing and resolving problems was to Geoffrey a destructive and carping challenge to authority. The differences were bridged, both sides offering protests and explanations and I myself for this single occasion intervening and acting as interpreter of one side to the other. But the episode demonstrates convincingly that the same procedures can carry very different meanings to participants.

Finally, to show how futile it is to attempt simple analyses of leader-member inter-actions, I shall give Lynda's later summary of the dancers' views on the kind of training sessions they wanted. The very group that was so anxious to explore, to question, to consult, wanted a decisively authoritarian approach in training classes. But, and this is the point, was not willing to accept this 'authority' from any of their own members because they had grown accustomed to mutual challenge in other roles. As teachers of children they wanted to be catalysts and facilitators. For the training of their own bodies in technique and in movement discipline, they wanted the security of authority, authority uncontaminated by any other role.

Lynda explained (note how the concept of 'teacher' in the training class differs from the concept of teaching they all exemplified in relation to children):

> We are giving each other classes and with the best will in the world you can't just become a teacher and have people obey you implicitly or look up to you as a teacher and accept what you say is right and wrong, when the day before you've been just one of the class and have been corrected yourself. We'd like someone from outside who wasn't one of us. A teacher, and what they say is wrong is wrong, and what they say is right is right, and if they say you're doing that wrong you have to accept it. Whereas if Fionna says it, for

instance, and I'm feeling cross with Fionna I think, 'Well, what do you know? I've had the same training as you.' Originally when we first came Fionna was going to be the teacher and not perform. That would have been fine. She would have been just the teacher.

'How would you have felt, though? Wouldn't you have said, "She's only had the same training?" '

LYNDA No. Not really because she's a better class teacher than I am—much better—no. That would have been all right.

So, for different tasks, members want different styles of leadership. And for the important technical task of body training, they want to have an unquestioning belief in the trainer's 'authority'. This, curiously enough, is not quite the same as a belief in the trainer's expertise. Fionna's expertise is unchanged in either situation. What changes is Lynda's response; she can only accept this discipline if the expertise has been unchallenged. By confining Fionna to a specific role, challenge would have been avoided.

Simple trait theories of leadership have long since been abandoned and the complexity of what constitutes effective leader behaviours have increasingly been recognised (Cartwright & Zander, 1960, introduction to Part Five). This survey of some of the decision-taking and problem-solving episodes experienced by the company has revealed the subtle inter-action of a range of complex factors in the field situation—the background assumptions of members, the emotionally-charged reciprocal reactions of leaders and followers in face to face groups, the nature of the tasks, the level of commitment, the differing interpretations of reality arrived at by individuals. Given these interacting elements, it is obvious that simple analyses which leave out members' interpretations are inadequate to cope with the factors involved. Departing from methodological considerations into prescriptions for action, it is equally obvious that leader-like behaviours must encompass a range of strategies to be effective. Leaders must be capable of being followers, since in any long-term group, company, team or class, opportunities will arise for all members to be both deciders and decision-acceptors. The official leader needs flexibility to adapt to differing expectations and to the differing requirements of differing tasks. In the dynamics of real-life situations any single type of leader behaviour will inevitably prove too rigid. It is important to avoid ideological stances. In social, work and classroom situations there is a temptation to opt for a broad concept: to advocate 'democratic' for instance, and to shun 'authoritarian'. In some situations the questioning, exploratory approach may undoubtedly be appropriate: in others a structured, decisive, explicit leadership may be needed. Official leaders should be aware of their own preferences and should have sufficient adaptability to encompass both. Members will wish to simplify their lives by type-casting: by investing one type of leadership in one person, another in another. In organisations this may prove convenient and may be institutionalised. In face to face groups it is always a limitation of range and growth potential and is to be resisted. The teacher, the team manager, the coach, the organiser, the expedition leader, anyone with responsibilities for decision taking in relation to small groups must be aware of the dangers of stereotyping. They must develop their own and members' capacities to respond to a range of decision-taking and problem-solving processes, for only by such a range can purposes other than trivial be effectively accomplished. Above all, leaders and members must have opportunities to share their interpretation of the social world so that, even if decisions are then challenged, the intentions behind them will be in some measure comprehensible and the responses will in some measure carry their intended meanings.

10

ENDINGS

Laboratory groups are arbitrary collections of individuals brought together for short-term tasks. Their dispersal at the end of the experimental situation is imbued with no special significance: hence 'endings' do not feature in the majority of studies on group processes. The only exception occurs in studies devoted to T, therapy and study groups on the Tavistock model, where reactions to the disbanding of the group have been described, notably by Richardson (1967). Yet, in real life situations, endings when recognised as such are as potent as, if not more potent than, beginnings. I say 'if recognised as such' because for many 'social relationships there are imperceptible comings together and insidious driftings apart. Certain aspects of social life, however, are recognised as having specific starting and ending points, and ceremonies and rituals have been devised to channel the powerful emotions engendered and to signify through a *rite de passage* society's recognition of the importance of the event. Learning to cope with less highly charged endings is a social skill that humans acquire through countless interactions. It cannot only be the ease of the gesture which ensures that the first communication baby is taught to make to the group is 'Bye-bye!'

All members of *Movable Workshop* apart from Stuart and Geoffrey had contracts which terminated in April, 1974. The last performance for the group before disbanding was at Pitlochry Festival Theatre on the afternoon of Saturday, 6 April. I had explained at the outset of the research that I would not be able to attend that performance because of an engagement undertaken before the research began. For that final occasion, as for the group's beginnings, I would depend on the accounts of participants. In order personally to experience the group towards the end of its life span, however, I arranged to go over to Glasgow the Saturday before, March 30th. The company was still working under intensive pressure, appearing daily at Glasgow schools and at the weekends rehearsing a new item to add to the Pitlochry repertoire, as well as reviving the full range of the old. Nevertheless, they agreed to come together for recording on the Saturday evening, the meeting to be in the flat temporarily rented by Fionna and Lynda. Although I insisted to both that my reason for providing the food and wine for the group was to save them expense, an anthropologist would have recognised the symbolism of my gesture on this, for me, last encounter.

The evening provided clear evidence of one important feature of groups; namely, that a group which knows the date of its ending is already preparing for dissolution before the actual event. Fionna had pointed out, in the tight cohesion of the tour, how in a new hotel individuals went from room to room for a reassuring check as to where everyone was. Now there was a sense of dispersal, a vagueness as to whereabouts. When I arrived Lynda was apparently alone in the flat. Shortly afterwards Peter came. We decided to go into a bedroom to set up the tape recorder so that I could record away from the main group. The door lock had jammed. A curious feature was that Lynda did not know whether Fionna was asleep inside—snatching sleep was rational under current pressures. We three called out to rouse her. No reply. In the end Peter—providentially the largest man in the company—threw himself at the door which needed to be opened in any case. At the third attempt the lock burst and he hurtled in. The room was empty. Shortly afterwards Fionna came in with Gary. Stuart arrived alone. Then Geoffrey. The rest, apart from Marita who was attending a wedding party, drifted in at different times. Lisa sat at one side of the room, rather isolated, Gavin at the opposite end. Bob arrived with a girl friend. I suggested that we eat first, then record. The recordings went on late. When I emerged after the interviews most of the group had unceremoniously gone their different ways.

Mills and Rosenberg (1970, p. 246) in analysing the life cycle of groups, assert that towards the end of the cycle:

> . . . the boundary between group members and others is dissolved by bringing friends in as visitors.

Bob, who had never been restricted by boundaries, was the one to breach it that evening. The presence of an outsider, the absence of Marita, the lack of co-ordination in arrivals and departures, the functional but symbolic breaking down of a door, seemed to signify that the group was already in the throes of preparing for dispersal.

In discussion it was apparent that attention was focused beyond Pitlochry to the period after the group's disbanding, described as a welcome return to normality:

GARY I don't really think about Pitlochry. When I think about the future now it's beyond that. I'll be really glad just to do something different whatever it is.

FIONNA That's all I can think about, getting back to normal.

There was some pleasure that the programme would have fresh elements, but a sense of strain at having to learn something new at this penultimate stage in the groups life.

'Is it a relief to be doing something new?'

PETER Extra strain.

FIONNA Strain—rushing through a new piece at this stage.

LYNDA It's quite nice, though, knowing we haven't just to go on and do *Caritas again*.

GARY,
PETER Yes, Yes.

GARY It will be a new programme. Just a few more performances of the old, thank God.

There was unease at the ambiguities of an unknown future:

GARY I get the feeling of insecurity. There are lots of possibilities but at the same time a lot of nothing afterwards—what's going to happen?'

Nevertheless there was no desire to cling to what was now over-familiar. Indeed there was a strong denial of any dependence on each other. When asked what they had gained from the experience 'Independence' was the term most frequently used:

GARY I'm more self-assured knowing I can get along—more independent.

FIONNA Having to perform every day—we've gained a lot from doing it. Being self-assured. I'm much more independent as a person now, which I enjoy in a way.

A sense of sour tiredness, however, of ambivalent and negative feeling, of need for reassurance came over strongly in spite of these claims for independence:

GARY It's a very insecure business, being an artist of any sort. But being a performer and going on stage, if you are not told this is all right, you're doing very well, you get a terrible suspicion that you are making a bloody fool of yourself going on stage every day—that you're doing something awful.

This desire for security and praise, however, was not

accompanied by any admission of inter-dependence on each other. Indeed, there was even a denial that there had been any intimacy of knowledge or of feeling within the group as a whole (though individual pairs admitted that they would miss each other):

> 'You made an interesting distinction, Gary. You said, "We don't know each other very well but we are familiar with each other." '

GARY Yes.
PETER Very true.

> 'Do you accept that distinction?'

GARY Yes.
FIONNA Yes. Acquaintances. Acquaintances.
GARY I mean this evening is very rare. We're getting on very well with each other tonight.

> 'For whose benefit?'

GARY For all of us.
FIONNA I always get the feeling that we're thrown together. We've got to work together, we've got to get on, so we do. I mean, we are forced to.

The reason for their coming together in the first place has been the dance:

GARY The dance has been the *raison d'etre* for so many things. There's been no other reason for us to be together.

Now the dance tour is nearing completion, and there is nothing else to hold them together, no reason why they should not separate with relief.

Ambivalence towards the task, a reluctance to admit to

feelings other than negative ones, a claim for independence and autonomy, a denial of close knowledge of each other except in unspecified pair groupings, these were the messages being communicated that evening. They seemed to me part of an understandable, indeed necessary, process of detachment to be worked through before the actual disbanding.

For Geoffrey and for Stuart, however, Pitlochry, though the end of one season, was merely a stage. For the previous fortnight they had been winding up the old while re-planning the new. They had discussed future career-possibilities with all the company apart from Gary and Fionna and were to talk with them before the week was out. Negotiations with Gulbenkien for a grant towards a musician for the next tour (Bob was returning to the University to complete his degree) were going on; arrangements for an American teacher to take the training classes were under way; Geoffrey was already making future bookings, including a tour of Northern Ireland and the Western Isles of Scotland. For them, endings were very much merged with beginnings, with Pitlochry a pivot between the two:

STUART It may give the whole thing a rather marvellous culmination if it goes well. And if it goes badly it will be an unfortunate end for them, and it will have repercussions for us—will set up a chain reaction. So we don't know, but then you never know. The one thing that is sure, is certain, is that their personalities will come across. Whether the works will stand up to the situation is another matter. This is my worry now, as artistic director.

I asked Stuart whether he felt, because he was planning the next tour, that this detached him to some extent:

It has to. When I hear them talking about their plans one feels in many ways that one is left behind. So I think you have to be a bit detached. The fact that I *am* left behind is of course what it's all about. It's very strange. It's like the very first time I waved goodbye to my family but then I was the one that was going. And so now it's the opposite. In life you are sometimes the person waving goodbye and sometimes the person going. At this moment in time I'm the person waving goodbye. There's the feeling that they are going off, and do I want to be going off also, you know?

'Is there a hint of envy, perhaps, that their future is as open?'

STUART No. I think actually I have accepted what I am doing and it has to be followed through. Otherwise there's no point. But just, just a hint of envy. Except that one has been through that and done those things. It's still near enough, though, to be just, just there. It's very fascinating, but I'm not enjoying it too much. I'm finding that in terms of age, suddenly, for the first time in my life I feel over thirty.

'What's made you feel this just now?'

I don't know. I suppose it's to do with my father, with the general process of ageing, commitments and responsibilities which one just did not have five or six years ago. It's only just now really hit me personally in the last couple of weeks.

When the children depart, parents feel their age. It is interesting that Stuart makes an analogy with family farewells that revived in my mind the family image used quite independently by several members earlier in the group's life. That image was now being obliquely and necessarily denied by everything the members said that evening. Stuart, however, who had never utilised it earlier, was now making the analogy. Possibly the extra maturity he was aware of and the detachment he claimed to have achieved made it possible for him to utilise it at this stage.

My first knowledge of the performance at Pitlochry came from reading the criticism in *The Guardian*. This was enthusiastic:

> On Saturday at Pitlochry Festival Theatre, the *Movable Workshop* Programme, performed for a first time in a formal theatre situation, was seen to be so effective, in a word so good, that it deserves many more public showings when the group reassemble next year.
>
> At first the picture—bare stage, plain white backdrop, grey tights and leotards and bare feet all round—seems austere, but not for long. These dancers have been chosen for outgoing personalities as well as talent. They are witty; they make immediate contact with the audience . . .

And so on to three paragraphs of unreserved praise.

Later came the accounts from the now dispersed company members. They provided a fascinating back-stage commentary. The performance had been not only highly successful, but chaotic and farcical. The stage at Pitlochry is very wide and shallow, and it was only possible to rehearse in it for a brief hour as a concert was held in the theatre that same morning. Lynda and Fionna, making an exit in the darkness after one item, had a violent collision, Lynda's eye being cut open and Fionna's cheek bruised. Later Marita, who had stepped so deftly around all the group pitfalls, fell into a physical hole off stage when looking for a chair. The audience was oblivious to this series of accidents and responded with enthusiasm, as did the critics.

Afterwards there had been a meal, champagne and gift-giving. Marita's and Lynda's fiancés had both been present, crossing the boundary and re-claiming for 'normality' two of the members. Then, emotional farewells.

These accounts were written and spoken after the event and after a period of reflection. It is interesting that at this stage it became possible for individuals, while expressing relief at escaping from membership, to acknowledge also their sense of loss and their positive feelings about the group:

GAVIN Quite naturally I felt pretty sad. I miss Gary, Lynda, Fionna, Peter, Marita, Stuart, Geoffrey, Lisa, Bob—I even miss that damn van. But I think after ten weeks of working it was nice that it all ended. It ended very cheerfully and happily. Everyone handed round presents and cried away to their heart's content. That was nice actually: I've known groups where the final parting was not so sweet as that one was. I think on the whole everyone did quite well—everyone gave just about as much as they could.

PETER Of course I was sad to say goodbye to the others, more so than I had expected. As a group of dancers, I felt we worked well with each other.

LYNDA One expects to feel an anticlimax, but it wasn't really that, just a wanting to get away and get back to normal. There was an excitement, too, at having done something well, and given our all to achieve that success. We were all sad to leave one another. Partings were a bit emotional, as they were bound to be since we'd been together for so long and through so much.

MARITA There is no doubt the group ended on a very successful and therefore happy note although not without mishap. We seemed to complement one another in our dancing and therefore something very rare happened in the dancing world and that is, we worked as a group.

GARY Okay, Pitlochry first. In some crazy way, I think it was the best performance *Movable Workshop* had ever done. But more importantly, it showed how well we worked together, submerging our own egos in the group identity (and this was something I didn't realise until Pitlochry). Perhaps it was simply that none of us felt individually strong enough as a dancer that we were all so content to let the group speak for us. Certainly off-stage we were far from being any sort of close unit (as you know). But at Pitlochry there were accidents, exhaustion, uncertainties to deal with. At the final performance everyone backstage was dancing with Peter in their minds as he did his *Handelabra* variation, giving him as much silent energy and encouragement as we could. When Marita couldn't find her chair and in her search for it fell into a hole offstage, we had to just go on, cover for her. Nobody freaked out, though what was to have been a thirty second oral improvisation lasted closer to five minutes. Though tired, we danced well. Stuart had properly taught us to let the choreography speak for itself, to dance accurately and intelligently. When it finally came time to do *Caritas* (after already dancing over an hour and a half) I just tried to be as accurate as possible, knowing I didn't have the strength for any bravura stunts. And in doing so, I realised that was how I should have been doing it all along.

Things got very emotional after the performance. I came off stage laughing and crying and hugged Stuart of all people. We got drunk on champagne in our dressing rooms and said how much we loved each other. Which was true. But we'd only just realised via that incredible performance.

Stuart had made his mental goodbyes the week before, in his image of waving farewell. The real goodbyes left him detached:

The ending was very happy—everyone very thrilled and relieved.

It was odd. I felt very outside it all and very distant watching everyone. It was as if I was a sympathetic bystander but not involved. I suppose professionally you develop a technique for dealing with goodbyes. The important thing isn't the moment of departure but what it has all been about, the whole tour. So in a way I wasn't moved by the departure. Geoffrey was. I don't think he has come so close to a group before. It was interesting that Marita was moved too. She is very professional but she felt that this particular group had something unique about it. But I knew that ultimately I should see them all again—the dance world is very small. Anyway, I know it is impossible to perpetuate things. Change is inevitable in the world of the theatre so you develop a sort of detachment. I didn't go out with the others to wave goodbye. I didn't feel any severing of the umbilical cord. For the dancers, as performers they had shared an experience of making theatre together, and what they share on stage in this way is very binding. A certain amount of isolation for me is inevitable. Geoffrey and I represent the continuity, though I don't know for how long.

Certain key processes are highlighted by this over-view of the final week of the group's life. First, group members prepare in advance for the period after disbanding. This is done consciously by attention to personal and career plans; at a less conscious level, individuals weaken the group's cohesion by crossing the boundary and inviting outsiders in. There is a denial of positive feeling except between members of sub-groups; a reluctance to admit the reality of the social world of the group which is instead disintegrated into fragmentary units. This process, though exacerbated in the dance company's case by the pressures of repetitive performances plus intensive rehearsals, is, I suggest, a necessary part of the business of re-establishing individual autonomy and detachment. This was particularly necessary with a group whose members had lived and worked in such close proximity over a ten week period. Once the group had disbanded, positive feeling could safely be acknowledged.

Those who represent continuity, as do teachers, lecturers, any individuals responsible for regular sequences of groups, acquire strategies for dealing with the sense of loss as one group departs. These strategies include the cultivation of a broad perspective, and the technique of planning for the new while still dealing with the old. Sometimes they include the denial of feeling, which may then manifest itself symbolically.

'The important thing isn't the moment of departure but what it has all been about.' This study will have made it apparent that there are no simple statements as to what it has all been about. But accepting the validity of conscious intention, part of what it has been about has been the stimulation of interest in dance in Scotland and the provision of opportunities to dance. Whether that stimulation and provision will prove to be a beginning of wider opportunities and participation cannot be predicted. *Movable Workshop* can be compared to a catalyst or to an evanescent display. Evidence contained in the appendix shows that, if the latter, at least it was not a damp squib. But a firework display gives at best brief illumination; a catalyst effects change. The intention behind the enterprise was to effect or strengthen innovation as was apparent from the type of items in the repertoire and from the utilisation of workshops. Innovation is dependent on two factors; first, the availability of the catalysing agent and second, the assimilation rather than rejection of change into the system. The continued existence of *Movable Workshop* as a catalysing agent is dependent on unstable resources. Funds must be provided from somewhere to cover the deficit between what the schools and colleges can pay for a visit, and the much higher costs of mounting the company. The extra funds have come from the main company's revenues, plus grants from funding organisations such as the Arts Council and Gulbenkien. The main company is likely to gain indirectly from the cultivation of an interest in dance among young people. There lie its future audiences. But the gain is long-term, indirect, and may be outweighed by more pressing considerations, such as the necessity in times of economic stringency to concentrate funds within a narrower spectrum, the necessity to concentrate talent within a single organisation with a recognisable house-style. Grants from Gulbenkien and the Arts Council are subject to changing priorities and to the current economic climate. The continuing availability of the catalysing agent is by no means certain.

Whether change is assimilated or rejected depends primarily on the meanings with which individual pupils, students, teachers and lecturers imbue their social worlds, and their interpretation of what is being offered by the catalysing agent. But, if acceptance follows, development and growth can only be sustained by appropriate structures. Those structures exist in the organisational networks of advisors and inspectors operating through the regions, in the varied provision for pre-service and inservice training offered by the colleges and universities, in the consultative functions of college lecturers and professional researchers, and in the supportive intervention of particular institutions as, in this instance, Dunfermline College. Bringing all this into enriching interplay with organisations from the very differing world of professional theatre is a complex task.

It is possible that this study may form part of the dialectic.

APPENDIX

As Others Saw Them

The group's interactions with schools and colleges was of a peculiar kind in that it was of high intensity and short duration. From the research angle, there was no developed inter-relation with other institutions to be explored. Nevertheless, the schools had a response to the dancers beyond the immediate applause and that response could be to some extent elucidated. Such elucidation would serve as a reminder of the broad context within which the group operated. It would also provide useful 'feedback' to the company, to organisers, teachers and lecturers which could be utilised in relation to further planning.

For the purpose of elucidation I decided to employ a postal questionnaire—'let every man be his own methodologist'—since there was no other economical way of gathering evidence from a range of institutions over a wide geographical area. The majority of questions were, however, open ended and categories were later deduced from a content analysis of replies, thus giving respondents as unstructured an opportunity as possible to express their reactions in their own terms.

The ensuing pamphlet was sent out to all the schools and institutions which had been visited by *Movable Workshop,* and is presented here exactly as dispatched to the participating teachers, lecturers, organisers etc. Its compilation and distribution invested my research role, retrospectively, with an authenticity and practical value which had not been immediately apparent to those who had encountered me sitting and watching from the side-lines in gyms, studios and school halls. Its circulation and, where read, assimilation will be an element in restructuring the social reality of *Movable Workshop's* subsequent tours.

Some Aspects of the Movable Workshops' Tour of Scotland

January 30th—April 6th, 1974

Introduction

In October, 1973, the *Movable Workshop* of Scottish Ballet Company agreed to collaborate with the Social Aspects Department of Dunfermline College of Physical Education in a research enterprise. This was to provide case material for a study in group dynamics. The field work ended in April 1974 and the research report will be available later in the year.

As an off-shoot of the main enquiry I felt it would be of interest both to the company and to the educational establishments visited, if some information could be collected as to the impact of the group's ten week tour of Scotland from January 30th-April 6th. The ensuing pamphlet is based on questionnaire replies from thirty-three secondary schools, a response rate of ninety-two per cent. A further section summarising the replies from six colleges and one university is included.

Slight variations occurred in the dance performance presented in the schools, not only because of the improvised nature of some sections of the programme but because certain items of the repertoire were omitted or included in the light of such factors as time available and the composition of the audience. The workshops showed even more variety because of the differing facilities and numbers of children involved. Thus in some schools as many as seventy-five children were taken as a total group, with resultant directed movement; in others there was subdivision into smaller units, with the children contributing their movement ideas. In spite of these differences I felt that there was a sufficient core of common experience to make the collection of information perfectly feasible. The resultant document testifies to the generous way in which respondents devoted time and thought to the questionnaire and particularly to the answering of the open-ended questions. The collaboration in the enterprise of the local advisers and the staffs of the various schools, colleges and universities visited by the *Movable Workshop* is greatly appreciated.

It will be obvious, then, that this pamphlet is offered not as a formal research report, but as a summary of information which will be of use both to the company and to the educational establishments. In this way I hope that it constitutes a practical expression of my appreciation to all concerned for their generous collaboration in the main enquiry.

Schools' Responses to the

Questionnaire

The first three questions asked for the name of the respondent, name of school and respondent's position in the school. As was to be expected, the visit of *Movable Workshop* had usually been made under the auspices of the Physical Education Department and the questionnaire was filled in by the Principal teacher of Physical Education, or colleagues in that department. In 9 schools, however, other staff members undertook the task. Three were filled in by Assistant Rectors, 2 by teachers in Art, 2 by Drama teachers, 1 by a Principal teacher, Guidance, and 1 by an English teacher.

Dance in the Schools

Question four asked for a brief indication as to whether any form of dance was taught in the school. The replies revealed that the majority of schools made provision for one or more of the following: Modern Educational Dance, National Dance, Scottish Country Dance, and Social. Thus only 3 of the 33 respondents replied that no dance of any kind was being taught, though in 2 more schools tuition was restricted to a

Scottish Country Dance Club or to sessions prior to social events.

In the remaining 28 schools some form of dance was taught as part of the official curriculum.

In 2 schools, one type: Modern Educational, recently started and restricted to 1st and 2nd year girls.

In 9 schools, two types: Modern Educational, plus Scottish, *or* National *or* Social.

In 14 schools, three types: Modern Educational, plus National/Scottish *or* National/Social *or* Social/Scottish.

In 3 schools, four types: Modern Educational, plus National/Scottish/Social.

Thus Modern Educational Dance receives the highest frequency of mention, being taught in 28 out of 33 schools. In spite of this, however, certain marked restrictions operate. Out of the 22 schools which specified an age range, 15 restricted the teaching to S1-S3. Only 7 schools stated that they offered it to a wider age range, 2 including all ages up to S6. Only 1 school specifically mentioned classes involving mixed groups and these were restricted to S1 and S2. With some brave exceptions the picture is predominantly of Modern Educational Dance as part of the curriculum for girls, particularly girls of the 11-14 age group. This situation, of course, arises not only from sex-typing within the Physical Educational curriculum (reflecting that in society at large) but from the different training backgrounds of men and women teachers of physical education.

The Value Placed on the Workshops and the Performances.

A minority of schools had arranged for either a workshop or a performance. The majority (28) had requested both. What is remarkable is the very positive response to both experiences recorded on the questionnaires.

Question 5 had asked the teachers to express their personal opinion of the workshop sessions on a five point scale ranging from 'extremely valuable' to 'of no value'.

9 classed the workshop as 'extremely valuable'
13 classed the workshop as 'very valuable'
7 classed the workshop as 'moderately valuable'

Only one respondent used the lower, negative end of the scale and classed the workshop as 'of little value' and no one utilised the 'no value' answer. With reference to the performance (Q.8) the positive response is even more marked, the corresponding figures being 10, 15 and 6, the lower end of the scale not being used at all. The evidence thus indicates a highly favourable response to both workshop and performance.

Because one person's response may be unrepresentative of the views of colleagues, opportunity was provided for recording differences of opinion (Qs. 6, 7 and 9). This was used on only two occasions, both with reference to the workshops. One school recorded that one teacher dissented from the 'very valuable' verdict of seven colleagues on the grounds that though the visit had been a welcome innovation, he was doubtful as to any lasting effect. In the second school the difference of opinion apparently arose from internal difficulties of organisation, in that volunteers were hard to find among the pupils so that the whole workshop concept posed problems. The highly favourable verdict recorded by individual teachers can thus be accepted as broadly representative of their colleagues' views.

This general approval is unmistakeably endorsed by the answer to Question 15. 'If a tour is organised for next year, would you wish the group to revisit the school?' On every questionnaire the reply was 'Yes'.

The Open-Ended Questions

The remaining section of the questionnaire consisted of open-ended questions which allowed the teachers to specify which aspects of the programme, if any, they considered most valuable and which, if any, they would wish to change. This freedom to express a wide range of opinion was deliberate, and in the covering letter teachers had been urged to be frank in their replies. The resulting information provided valuable insights with sufficient overlap of opinion to make categorisation possible. Because of the varied nature of the workshops a few answers were idiosyncratic. For example, one respondent appreciated the opportunity of being involved in a workshop for teachers:

> The staff session was very valuable because it enabled the sceptics to 'experience' dance,

but this was an opportunity utilised in only one area. Such single replies have not usually been referred to, except when they seemed of special interest. Instead, content analysis and categorisation have been employed to reveal shared opinions. The answer of any one person could, of course, cover a range of aspects, and where this occurred each point was classified within its appropriate category.

The Workshops

'What aspects of the workshop, if any, did you consider to be particularly valuable?' (Q. 11)

The direct participation of all the dancers in the workshop sessions was the element which received the highest number of appreciative references. Fourteen teachers referred to the stimulus and guidance this provided. The children were motivated by the excitement of participating with professionals, were challenged by the standard of performance and were encouraged by the friendly contact.

Typical replies are as follows:

> The fact that the children saw perfectionists at work seemed to make them strive to emulate the dancers.
>
> Watching good dancers in action is most stimulating to pupils and staff.
>
> I liked the way all the dancers joined in and helped the children.
>
> The personal contact of the dancers with small groups of children—this enabled them to produce more work, especially in an hour's session.

The next most valued element in terms of frequency of mention was *the musical accompaniment to the workshop sessions*. Classes had been intrigued and stimulated by the variety of sounds utilised; vocal, flute, electric organ and varied percussion. Ten respondents singled out this aspect:

> The children were introduced to new instrument sounds.
>
> Marvellous use of percussion.
>
> The interesting use of rhythm and live accompaniment.

I have termed another element in the replies '*the technical aspect*'. Included under this heading are seven appreciative comments. Four of these refer to the warm up material; the others praise the sense of structure and the fact that the movement was disciplined and demanded effort:

The stress placed on the value of warm up.
The work the children was given was taxing, difficult and demanded their full concentration.
The demonstration of technique.

Balancing these were five replies which could be categorised as stressing the more *creative, spontaneous element*. The opportunities given in some of the workshops for the children to create part of a dance were mentioned appreciatively by three teachers, and the sense of enjoyment and freedom from inhibitions by two others:

Help was given to pupils to work out their own ideas.
The part where the children themselves created part of a dance.
Interested pupils had a chance to work outside the inhibitions of a class situation.

As a further contrast to the stress on technical standards two teachers commented on the *width of appeal of the material* offered in the sessions, claiming that it had been enjoyed by children of widely varying ability:

Catered for both experienced and inexperienced dancers.
Children of all ability groups thoroughly enjoyed the workshop.

Finally two teachers appreciated the fact that the content of the workshops provided *new ideas and movement material* which could be related to school work.

'What aspects of the workshop, if any, would you wish to be changed or modified?' (Q. 12)

A striking tribute to the interest generated by the workshops is the fact that under 'modifications' the one that receives the highest frequency of mention is 'More Time'. Ten teachers would have appreciated longer sessions, an increase in the number of sessions to allow a wider range of children to be involved, or more time outside the sessions for the school staff to discuss the work with the dancers:

More time should be allocated and more pupils involved.

Within the time limit the workshop was, I think, very good, but much more time is required and I think that more than one session would greatly increase the value.

More time for discussion between staff and the group without a reduction in the movement time.

All these answers convey a clear desire for an extension of the movement experience sampled in the workshop.

As to the actual movement content of the workshops the most clearly expressed wish was for *more opportunities for the children to contribute to the movement ideas and the creation of dances.* We have seen from 3 favourable mentions earlier in the report that in those schools where this type of session was offered, the opportunity was appreciated. Under modifications, 7 teachers would have liked the workshops to have been less directed and to have provided more scope for the children to develop their own ideas and to participate in a culminating dance experience:

The children could have been given some opportunity to invent movement themselves instead of being directed all the time.

More dance, less directed movement.

Should have liked some end result or total 'rounding off' or 'tying up of work'.

Linked with this is a request from 5 teachers for opportunities to *subdivide into smaller groups:*

If the time were available I should like to see more group work.

Working with several leaders in smaller groups.

Two respondents suggested that perhaps the *stimuli could be varied,* possibly with the inclusion of improvised costume. It is apparent from all these replies that when modifications in content are suggested, it is in the direction of providing more scope for the children to develop ideas and make their own contribution to the total movement experience. The emphasis on time factors and on small groups reveals that teachers are well aware that both these elements are crucial in exploratory work of this kind.

A single plea, which may find echoes in others too discreet to write it:

Men to wear trousers rather than tights!

Five schools suggested no modifications.

The Performance

'What aspects of the dance performance, if any, did you consider to be particularly valuable?' (Q. 13)

One enthusiastic respondent refused to specify and wrote 'All of it'. Content analysis of the remaining questionnaires once again revealed overlap of opinion which made categorisation possible.

I have classed together all those replies which commented appreciatively on elements in the performance which made it *a learning experience* for the audience. There were 24 of these, an impressive total. Obviously the teachers had welcomed the fact that the performance was devised to give insights into the process of creating and performing dances. Appreciative reference was made to the explanations given before the dances were performed, and to the way dances were built up from individual motifs and improvised shapes. Six teachers particularly mentioned the way in which the use of sounds and rhythms had been demonstrated as an element in choreography:

The piece choreographed and danced 'there and then' was most enlightening.

Items which showed how the dancers started, selected and developed their own ideas into a whole.

I found the part where the company built up a dance on the stage most valuable.

Showed very clearly the relationship between music/voice sounds and movement.

A further element in the performance which was commented on with approval was *the interaction between the dancers and the audience.* There were 11 references to the way in which the dancers came across as individuals and drew the audience into direct participation in the programme, thus bridging the barrier between performers and spectators:

> The encouragement of audience participation which led to a feeling of knowing the dancers as individuals rather than remote performers.

> Speedy relationship built up between group and audience to get audience participation.

> Audience participation in music and rhythm-making.

Another cluster of references, 8, can be best classified as expressing appreciation of *the standard of performance.* This is an unspecified element in that enthusiasm for the quality of what was offered by the group is diffused over the entire programme and tends to be expressed in general terms:

> Excellent performance—well conceived imaginative and highly entertaining.

> The performance by the company was most enjoyable. The girls were really impressive. The audience realised that the simplest things could be performed with perfection.

> We have nothing but enthusiastic praise here, appearance, costume, lighting—immensely pleasing and exciting. Complete range of dance ideas—from instant individual improvisation to the utterly professional dance.

I grouped a further 8 references together because they praised elements which I have termed *approachability*: the ways in which the company made dance seem not a remote esoteric art but something to be enjoyed by all members of their audiences. This was achieved by such features as humour, the variety of work offered and the use in some items of contemporary 'pop' music:

They showed that dance was to be enjoyed and was at times amusing.

The fact that the group performed a dance to a modern record (Cat Stevens) which brought the dance nearer to the children's own imagination of what they would like to dance to, themselves.

The modern, up-to-date music, costume and dance ideas were pleasing to the children.

'What aspects of the dance performance, if any, would you wish to be changed or modified?' (Q. 14)

A sign of satisfaction is the fact that no fewer than 19 schools offered no suggestions for modification!

Six teachers felt that one or two of the dances had been rather difficult for the children to respond to. These were not named by reference to the programme, but were referred to as the 'unaccompanied' or 'abstract' ones. Four would have liked the omission of the more obscure dances from the programme. Two would have liked *more explanation* offered:

The unaccompanied sequence had little appeal for the pupils.

Although I would not like to see the more complicated dances omitted from the performance I think a fuller explanation could be given to help understand the meaning behind some of the dances.

The other modification put forward in 5 replies was for *more of the longer costumed pieces* to be included so that children could experience 'the magic of the theatre':

Perhaps more complete dances could have been shown. It was slightly stilted because of short training sketches. The children loved to see the longer dances and they saw only two.

Only when costume was used was 'the magic of the theatre' realised. Several pupils have remarked on this aspect, picking out the costumed items most favourably.

Perhaps the 1 person who requested a *longer programme* was thinking that this would allow for the inclusion of a greater number of fully developed dances.

General Comments

'Please include below any general comments prompted by the visit of the group.' (Q. 16)

It is not always possible to anticipate which elements in an experience will prove significant to the participants. The inclusion of a request for general comments was to ensure that the teachers had every chance to raise the issues which seemed important to them. Not all respondents utilised this opportunity: obviously in the rest of the questionnaire they had covered everything they wished to say. Twenty-eight teachers, however, offered further statements. It is interesting that not one of these was negative or denigratory in any way. One respondent made the quite legitimate point that:

'P.E. trained women who have had dance instruction (most of my staff) learned nothing new'

but this was on a questionnaire where the workshop had been classed as 'very valuable'.

Indeed many teachers used the section as a means of reiterating general approval:

The performance presented an image of ballet as a vivid, virile, colourful and expressive medium.

Excellent in all aspects.

Some of the statements strengthened information already recorded under earlier sections. Thus the personalities of the dancers, which had been praised in Q. 13 as registering with the audience, received further appreciative comments from 10 respondents:

> The delightful personalities of the dancers immediately captured the children's attentions and quickly interested them in their performances.

> This group was extremely pleasant, well mannered and very ready to discuss any aspect of the dance which interested or puzzled us.

> The dancers were very friendly and had an extremely good manner with children.

Obviously some special quality of the experience provided by *Movable Workshop* was dependent on the particular personalities of the company dancers and their ease in establishing contact with teachers and children.

The key issue of the complex relationship between the visit of the group and the ongoing work of the school was illumined by 10 comments. A session of a day or half a day is bound to have the character of a special event, and it is a matter of quite legitimate debate to question if such an experience can be integrated into ongoing work and to wonder what, if any, long term benefits are likely to accrue. Although the teachers must have been fully aware of all the problems of 'follow up', nevertheless 10 respondents used this section to state their belief that the visit had had beneficial effects on ongoing work. Seven replies referred to ways in which the workshops and performance had stimulated enthusiasm for the dance already offered in the school curriculum:

> I felt the workshop was a great boost to the enthusiasm for dance in the school, causing a great deal of renewed interest in the dance classes.

Dance is already popular in the school, but after the visit from the Scottish Theatre Ballet this added further interest and also set them off making all sorts of unusual percussion instruments.

Of very particular interest were 3 replies which indicated that the visit had strengthened the possibility of innovation:

The group's visit certainly inspired us and prompted a request from the pupils for a dance club after school.

Our pupils were inspired by the visit of the group and I and my staff were similarly motivated. In fact, at this present moment in time, I am endeavouring to set up a block of 6 weeks dance (Mod Ed) for boys of S1 and S2 next year, purely on an experimental basis.

The fact that the dancers were prepared to hold a workshop session for the Rugby XV was much appreciated and the Principal PE teacher thought it was a valuable session. The boys themselves, after initial reluctance, participated well and enjoyed the session. Personally I feel that more of this type of session with boys participating would do much to lessen the considerable prejudice felt regarding male dancers by the majority of boys.

It is maybe too soon to say how much of a contribution has resulted from the visit. The Drama Club must surely have benefited and some art pupils took advantage of the visit to make drawings which have been used since for composition and modelling.

In view of the favourable nature of all the comments offered, it is only to be expected that 2 teachers regretted that more children had not been able to share the experience, 2 wished for more frequent visits and 1 would have liked more time to talk to the dancers. Two felt that more information in advance of the performance would have been helpful in informing colleagues of the kind of learning experience which was being provided and in selecting pupils for the workshops:

To end on a down-to-earth note. One teacher remarked:

> It would be desirable (although not necessarily possible) to see more than 1 lesson—a series—to show some sort of progression of work and improvement in quality.

This statement surely implies a recognition of the day to day task still left for the teachers to tackle after the *Movable Workshop* has packed its hampers and its equipment and driven away.

Responses from Institutions
of Higher Education

Movable Workshop visited six colleges and three universities in the course of the tour. These were informed of the questionnaire which had been sent to the schools and were invited to supply supplementary evidence by filling in a similar document. The six colleges and one university responded. Because of the maturity of the audiences and the increased number and length of the workshop sessions I decided it was appropriate to present this material separately.

What is impressive, however, is the way in which responses from these institutions largely parallel the responses from the schools. Obviously the group's programme was of sufficient adaptability and range to interest students and teachers at their own levels. Thus, in evaluating the workshops, 5 respondents classed them as extremely valuable, 1 as very valuable, 1 as moderately valuable. The corresponding figures for the performance were 3, 1 and 2 (one college did not arrange for a performance). The lower negative end of the scale was not used. Only 2 differences of opinion were recorded. One lecturer felt that the workshop (classed by his colleagues as extremely valuable) would have gained from some demonstration work which would have helped a group of students who were reluctant to put forward suggestions. In relation to the dance performance, 1 respondent who classed it as moderately valuable because it was less experimental than she had anticipated, recorded that the rest of her colleagues felt it had been extremely valuable.

So again, as with the schools, a strong consensus of very positive feeling emerges, which is confirmed by the fact that every institution wished for a return visit from the group.

The workshops in these colleges and universities varied very considerably in length and purpose. Nevertheless, most of the comments on what was specially valued fell within the categories established in relation to the schools' replies.

Three comments mentioned the *creative aspects,* the insights into choreography and the satisfaction arising from the creation of dance.

Three comments mentioned the *direct participation of all the dancers* and the personal contact established.

Two comments mentioned the *musical accompaniment to the workshop sessions.*

One comment mentioned the *technical aspects,* the 'disciplined basis'. An additional comment praised 'the clarity in presentation i.e. a learning experience was followed by practice using the material previously taught.'

A clear indication of satisfaction is that 5 respondents suggested no modifications at all. One would have liked longer sessions, and 1 a greater range of dance styles and choreographic techniques.

In relation to the performance, what was valued was once again the *interaction between the dancers and the audience* (3 references) and the *standard of performance* (1 reference):

'The high standard of execution: the life and vitality of the dancers.' However, since these were adult audiences, 3 respondents particularly singled out 'theatrical dances' or 'more professional items' as having the greatest appeal. The strong emphasis the schools placed on those elements in the programme which made it a learning experience was not repeated here.

Instead, under modifications, suggestions centred on ways of strengthening the performance as a learning situation for these more experienced adults. Thus 2 respondents would have liked a greater range of material and technique, 1 a deeper exploration of movement relationships. Though 1 lecturer felt that the 'abstract dance' (singled out for praise by another) should have been omitted, another respondent asked for greater experiment and risk-taking provided it was in the context of discussion.

Under general comments, once again the personalities of the dancers were singled out for particular praise. One lecturer felt that the dancers' teaching skills had made the workshops better than the performance; another showed appreciation for both aspects of what they offered:

> Altogether extremely satisfying. The dancers were praised for their ability to relate so well to the students in the workshop sessions, and to perform with such a high degree of skill such a short time after.

As with the schools, there emerged a strongly expressed belief in the value of the interaction between professionals and the educational establishments. The encounters generated great enthusiasm and provided a stimulus for innovation:

> Students reactions were highly enthusiastic. Most of them would have enjoyed a follow up in terms of more workshop sessions and discussion.
>
> The men students were slightly apprehensive about 'dance sessions' but were fully converted by the end of the afternoon. They were very enthusiastic about it afterwards. We have had enquiries from them about further dance classes and two students incorporated workshop exercises in a P.E. programme they devised for a Parents' Day in a Primary School.
>
> The choreography evolved in the workshop was remarkably sophisticated. We have drawn the conclusion that in our practical courses there is a permanent place for long sessions of this kind with visiting expert groups.

Finally to quote one lecturer from an area which had experienced 2 performances ('73 and '74) and 3 workshops. He described the interesting local developments in dance, culminating in three hundred children from twelve schools showing their work:

> There is a growing *demand* for these workshops which have played such a big role in these developments.

Concluding Remarks

The information collected in this pamphlet, is as explained in the introduction, peripheral to a research enquiry which has a quite different focus. Because of this I am very conscious of what the document does not set out to do. It does not constitute an investigation into the position of dance in Scottish schools, into the curriculum objectives, into the children's attitude to the subject, into the problems and rewards of teaching dance at secondary level, and into the factors involved in successful curriculum innovation. These topics would justify a full scale research undertaking in their own right.

What the document does offer is information as to the impact of a particular group of dancers on a wide range of schools and institutions of higher education. That the response was highly positive is apparent from the evidence mustered. The group was perceived as offering not only an experience which was very stimulating and enjoyable on the day, but one with beneficial repercussions extending beyond the specific workshops and performance.

The high value placed by the teachers on the interaction between this professional group and the educational establishments visited is apparent from their responses on the five point scale. The direct quotations from school and college staff may stimulate discussion and reflection not only about the visit of *Movable Workshop* but even about the position of the arts in education and in national culture.

EDITH COPE

June 1974

THE MOVABLE WORKSHOP
PRESENTED BY
SCOTTISH THEATRE BALLET

The Company:

PETER ALLAN	FIONNA MCPHEE
G. W. COBB	BOB STUCKEY
LYNDA COLSTON	MARITA WEST

Programme devised and directed by
STUART HOPPS

Costumes designed and made by — Alan   Alexander   and David Beaton

Electronic music recorded by — courtesy of Glasgow University Electronic Studios

PROGRAMME

'WHAT ARE YOU DOING?'
Preparation in order to begin

DANCE BY ADDITION
Creating a dance by individual contribution from the dancers

RHYTHMS
Composing rhythmic patterns and developing them into a dance

SHAPE
Discovering body shapes and grouping them into dance patterns

Interval

1. *HANDELABRA*	*Music:*	Handel
	Choreography:	Stuart Hopps

2. *GONE*	*Music:*	Stuckey
	Choreography:	G. W. Cobb
3. *CHARADE*	*Music:*	Britten
	Choreography:	Larry McKinnon/ Rosemary Martin
4. *ZODIAC*	*Music:*	Stuckey
	Choreography:	Bob Stuckey
5. *SO ANYWAY*	*Music:*	Meredith Monk
	Choreography:	Larry McKinnon
6. *UNEVEN TIME*	*Choreography:*	Rosemary Martin
7. *THE GIRL WITH THE FLAXEN HAIR*	*Music:*	Debussy
	Choreography:	Stuart Hopps
8. *CARITAS*	*Music:*	Cat Stevens
	Choreography:	Peter Darrell

MOVABLE WORKSHOP is the name given to the new modern dance touring group of Scottish Theatre Ballet, under the direction of Stuart Hopps, the Associate Director of Scottish Theatre Ballet. Movable Workshop tours schools colleges and art centres with a series of informal lecture demonstrations and performances as well as creating workshops in which students and their teachers may participate.

Movable Workshop also tours to other venues where—because of stage limitations—the main company are unable to appear. The group made their inaugural appearance in the joint production by Scottish Theatre Ballet with the Traverse Theatre, Edinburgh, of the Scots author C. P. Taylor's play 'Columba' in Edinburgh last Christmas.

For Movable Workshop:

Stage Manager	GAVIN DRUMMOND
Wardrobe Mistress	ELIZABETH HAMILL

For Scottish Theatre Ballet:

Chairman	ROBIN DUFF
Director	PETER DARRELL
Associate Director	STUART HOPPS
Administrator	ROBIN ANDERSON
Assistant Administrator	GEOFFREY McNAB
Scottish Theatre Ballet Ltd.	

REFERENCES

Allport, F. H. *Social Psychology*. Boston: Houghton Mifflin, 1924.

Ardray, R. *The Territorial Imperative*. New York: Atheneum, 1966.

Argyle, M. *Social Interaction*. London: Methuen, 1969.

Argyle, M. *The Social Psychology of Work*. Harmondsworth: Penguin, 1974.

Argyle, M. & Lee, V. *Social Relationships*. Bletchley: Open University Press, 1972.

Aronson, E. & Mills, T. Effect of severity of initiation on liking for a group. In D. Cartwright & A. Zander (Eds.) *Group Dynamics. Research and Theory*. London, Tavistock, 1960.

Bales, R. F. *Interaction Process Analysis: A Method for the Study of Small Groups*. Reading, Mass: Addison-Wesley, 1950.

Bales, R. F. The equilibrium problem in small groups. In T. Parsons, R. F. Bales & E. A. Shils (Eds.) *Working Papers in the Theory of Action*. New York: Free Press, 1953.

Bales, R. F. & Slater, P. E. Role differentiation in small decision-making groups. In T. Parsons & R. F. Bales (Eds.) *Family, Socialization and Interaction Process*. New York: Free Press, 1955.

Barber, B. Some problems in the sociology of the professions. *Daedalus* A. A. A. S. Jnl., 1963, **92**, 669–688.

Bavelas, A. Leadership: man and function. In C. A. Gibb (Ed.) *Leadership*. Harmondsworth: Penguin, 1969.

Becker, H. *Outsiders: Studies in the Sociology of Deviancy*. London: Collier-Macmillan, 1963.

Benthall, J. & Polhemus, T. (Eds.) *The Body as a Medium of Expression*. London: Allen Lane, 1975.

Berger, P. & Kellner, H. Marriage and the construction of reality. In H. P. Dreitsel (Ed.) *Recent Sociology No. 2*. London: Collier-Macmillan, 1970.

Bion, W. R. *Experiences in Groups*. London: Tavistock, 1961.

Bosmajian, H. A. (Ed.). *The Rhetoric of Non-Verbal Communication*. London: Scott, Foresman, 1971.

Bottomore, T. B. *Elites and Society*. London: C. A. Watts, 1964.

Brown, J. A. C. *The Social Psychology of Industry*. Harmondsworth: Pelican, 1954.

Calhoun, J. B. Population density and social pathology. *Scientific American*, 1962, 206, 139–50.

Carter, L., Haythorn, W., Shriver, B. & Lanzetta, J. The behaviour of leaders and other group members. In D. Cartwright & A. Zander (Eds.) *Group Dynamics. Research and Theory*. London: Tavistock, 1960.

Cartwright, D. & Zander, A. (Eds.) *Group Dynamics. Research and Theory*. London: Tavistock, 1960 (2nd ed.).

Cicourel, A. *Method and Measurement in Sociology*. New York: Free Press, 1964.

Coser, L. A. *The Functions of Social Conflict*. London: Routledge & Kegan Paul, 1965.

Curl, G. The skilful—a major sector of the aesthetic. *The Laban Art of Movement Guild Magazine*, Nov. 1974, 27–46.

Deutsch, M. A theory of co-operation and competition. *Human Relations*, 1949, **2**, 129–52.

Durkheim, E. *Professional Ethics and Civil Morals*, trans. C. Brookfield. London: Routledge & Kegan Paul, 1957.

Elias, N. & Dunning, E. Dynamics of sport groups with special reference to football. In E. Dunning (Ed.) *The Sociology of Sport*. London: Frank Cass, 1971.

Emerson, Joan. Behaviour in private places: sustaining definitions of reality in gynaecological examinations. In H. P. Dreitzel (Ed.) *Recent Sociology No. 2*. London: Collier-Macmillan, 1970.

Etzioni, Amitai. *Modern Organizations,* Englewood Cliffs: Prentice-Hall, 1964.

Fiedler, F. E. Leadership—a new model. In C. A. Gibb (Ed.) *Leadership.* Harmondsworth: Penguin, 1969.

Filmer, P. Philipson, M., Silverman, D. & Walsh, David. *New Directions in Sociological Theory.* London: Collier-Macmillan, 1972.

Freud, S. Group psychology and the analysis of the ego. In *The Complete Psychological Works.* London: Hogarth, 1953-64.

Garfinkel, H. *Studies in Ethnomethodology.* Englewood Cliffs: Prentice-Hall, 1967.

Gibb, C. A. (Ed.) *Leadership.* Harmondsworth: Penguin, 1969.

Goffman, E. *The Presentation of the Self in Everyday Life.* New York: Doubleday Anchor, 1959.

Goffman, E. *Asylums.* New York: Doubleday Anchor, 1961.

Goffman, E. *Relations in Public.* New York: Basic Books, 1971.

Gorer, G. *Africa Dances.* Harmondsworth: Penguin, 1945.

Hall, E. T. Proxemics. *Current Anthropology*, 1968, **9**, 83-95.

Hare, A. P., Borgatta, E. P. & Bales, R. F. (Eds.) *Small Groups: Studies in Social Interaction.* New York: Knopf, 1955.

Harré, R. & Secord, P. F. *The Explanation of Social Behaviour.* Oxford: Blackwell, 1972.

Hinde, R. A. *Non-verbal Communication.* London: Cambridge University Press, 1972.

Homans, G. C. *The Human Group.* London: Routledge & Kegan Paul, 1951.

Horner, A. & Buhler, C. Existential and humanistic psychology. *International Psychiatry Clinics*, 1969, **6**, 55-73.

Jennings, H. H. Sociometric differentiation of the psyche group and the sociogroup. *Sociometry,* 1947, **10**, 71-79.

Johnson, T. J. *Professions and Power.* London: Macmillan, 1972.

Jourard, S. M. *The Transparent Self.* London: Van Nostrand Reinhold Company, 1971.

Kelsall, R. K. *Higher Civil Servants in Britain from 1870 to the Present Day.* London: Routledge & Kegan Paul, 1955.

Laban, R. *Modern Educational Dance.* London: Macdonald & Evans, 1948.

Laing, R. D. *The Politics of Experience and the Bird of Paradise.* Harmondsworth: Penguin, 1967.

Langer, Susanne K. *Feeling and Form.* London: Routledge & Kegan Paul, 1953.

Lenk, H. Top performance despite internal conflicts. In J. W. Loy & G. S. Kenyon (Eds.) *Sport, Culture and Society*. New York: Macmillan, 1969.

Lewin, K., Lippit, R. & White, R. Patterns of aggressive behaviour in experimentally created 'social climates'. *Journal of Social Psychology*, 1939, **10**, 271-99.

Lewin, K. *Resolving Social Conflicts*. New York: Harper & Row, 1948.

Loy, J. W. & Kenyon, G. S. *Sport, Culture and Society*. New York & London: Collier-Macmillan, 1969.

MacIver, R. M. & Page, C. H. *Society: an Introductory Analysis*. London: Macmillan, 1950.

Marx, K. Theories of Surplus Value. (Vol. IV of *Capital*) trans. Emile Burns. London: Lawrence & Wishart, 1969.

Maslow, A. *Motivation and Personality*. New York: Harper & Brothers, 1954.

Maslow, A. *Towards a Psychology of Being*. New Jersey: Van Nostrand, 1962.

Mayo, E. The Political Problem of an Industrial Civilisation. Appendix to *The Social Problems of an Industrial Civilisation*. London: Routledge & Kegan Paul, 1949.

McFeat, Tom. *Small Group Cultures*. New York: Pergamon Press, 1974.

McGrath, Joseph E., & Altman, Irwin. *Small Group Research*. New York: Holt, Rinehart & Winston 1966.

Mead, G. H. *Mind, Self and Society*. Chicago: University of Chicago Press, 1934.

Mead, Margaret. *Continuities in Cultural Evolution*. New Haven: Yale University Press, 1965.

Merleau-Ponty, M. Phenomenology and the sciences of man. In J. O'Neill, (Ed.) *Phenomenology, Language and Sociology*. London: Heinemann, 1974.

Miller, E. J. & Rice, A. K. *Systems of Organisation: The Control of Task & Sentient Boundaries*. London: Tavistock, 1967.

Millerson, G. *The Qualifying Associations: A Study in Professionalisation*. London: Routledge & Kegan Paul, 1964.

Mills, C. Wright. *The Sociological Imagination*. New York: Oxford University Press, 1959.

Mills, T. M. & Rosenberg, S. (Eds.) *Readings on the Sociology of Small Groups*. Englewood Cliffs: Prentice-Hall, 1970.

Mitchell, Duncan G. (Ed.) *A Dictionary of Sociology*. London:

Routledge & Kegan Paul, 1968.

Moreno, J. L. *Who Shall Survive?* Washington D.C.: Nervous & Mental Diseases Publishing Co., 1934.

Morris, D. The response of animals to a restricted environment. *Symposium Zoological Society, London*, 1964, **13**, 99-118.

Murray, E. J. *Motivation and Emotion*. Englewood Cliffs: Prentice-Hall, 1964.

O'Neill, J. *Sociology as a Skin Trade*. London: Heinemann, 1972.

Parsons, T., Shils, E. A. & Olds, J: Values, motives and systems of action. In T. Parsons & E. A. Shils (Eds.) *Towards a General Theory of Action*. Cambridge, Massachusetts: Harvard University Press, 1951.

Parsons, T. Professions. In *The International Encyclopaedia of the Social Sciences*. London: Collier-Macmillan, 1968.

Polanyi, Michael. *Personal Knowledge: Towards a Post-Critical Philosophy*. London: Routledge, 1958.

Pym, D. In quest of post-industrial man. In N. Armistead (Ed.) *Reconstructing Social Psychology*. Harmondsworth: Penguin, 1974.

Richardson, Elizabeth. *The Environment of Learning*. London: Nelson, 1967.

Richardson, Elizabeth. *Group Study for Teachers*. London: Routledge & Kegan Paul, 1967.

Rowan, J. Research as intervention. In N. Armistead (Ed.) *Reconstructing Social Psychology*. Harmondsworth: Penguin, 1974.

Rueschemeyer, D. Doctors and lawyers. A comment on the theory of the professions. *Canadian Review of Sociology and Anthropology*, 1964, **1**, 17-30.

Russell, Joan. *Modern Dance in Education*. London: Macdonald & Evans, 1958.

Rust, Frances. *Dance in Society*. London: Routledge & Kegan Paul, 1969.

Sachs, C. *World History of Dance*. New York: Norton, 1937.

Shaw, M. E. Communication networks, In P. B. Smith (Ed.) *Group Processes*. Harmondsworth: Penguin, 1970.

Sherif, M. *Group Conflict and Co-operation*. London: Routledge & Kegan Paul, 1966.

Sherwood, M. Bion's experiences in groups. A critical evaluation. *Human Relations*, 1964, **17**, 113-29.

Silverman, David. *The Theory of Organizations*. London: Heinemann, 1972.

Simmel, George. *The Sociology of George Simmel*. Trans. K. H.

Wolff. Glencoe; Free Press, 1950.

Sommer, R. Further studies in small group ecology. In J. Laver & S. Hutcheson (Eds.) *Communication in Face to Face Interaction*. Harmondsworth: Penguin, 1972.

Taylor, L. & Williams, Kate. The actor and his world. *New Society*, 1971, **29,** 188–90.

Tönnies, F. J. & Loomis, C. P. *Fundamental Concepts in Sociology*. New York: American Book Co, 1940.

Trist, E. L., Higgin, G. W., Pollock, A. E., Murray, A. H. Sociotechnical Systems in P. B. Smith (Ed.) *Group Processes* Harmondsworth: Penguin, 1970.

Tuckman, B. W. Developmental sequences in small groups. In P. B. Smith (Ed.) *Group Processes*. Harmondsworth: Penguin, 1970.

Verba, S. *Small Groups and Political Behaviour, a Study of Leadership*. New Jersey: Princeton University Press, 1961.

Von Wiese, L. & Becker, H. *Systematic Sociology*. New York & London: John Wiley, 1932.

Walsh, D. Sociology and the social world. In P. Filmer et al. *New Directions in Sociological Theory*. London: Collier-Macmillan, 1972.

Weber, M. *The Theory of Social and Economic Organization*. New York: Free Press, 1964.

White, R. & Lippit, R. Leader behaviour and member reaction in three 'social climates'. In D. Cartwright & A. Zander (Eds.) *Group Dynamics. Research and Theory*. London: Tavistock, 1960.

Whyte, W. F. *Street Corner Society*. Chicago: University of Chicago Press, 1943.

CONTENT INDEX

AUTHOR INDEX

KING ALFRED'S COLLEGE
LIBRARY